real-life
discipleship

training manual

equipping disciples who
make disciples

real-life
discipleship

training manual

jim putman // avery t. willis jr. // brandon guindon // bill krause

NAVPRESS
Discipleship Inside Out®

NavPress is the publishing ministry of The Navigators, an international Christian organization and leader in personal spiritual development. NavPress is committed to helping people grow spiritually and enjoy lives of meaning and hope through personal and group resources that are biblically rooted, culturally relevant, and highly practical.

**For a free catalog go to www.NavPress.com
or call 1.800.366.7788 in the United States or 1.800.839.4769 in Canada.**

ISBN-13: 978-1-61521-559-1

Cover design by Studio Gearbox
Cover images by Veer, iStock, Getty, Masterfile, and Photo.com

Some of the anecdotal illustrations in this book are true to life and are included with the permission of the persons involved. All other illustrations are composites of real situations, and any resemblance to people living or dead is coincidental.

Unless otherwise identified, all Scripture quotations in this publication are taken from the *Holy Bible, New International Version*® (NIV®). Copyright © 1973, 1978, 1984 by International Bible Society. Used by permission of Zondervan. All rights reserved. Other versions used include: the New American Standard Bible® (NASB), Copyright © 1960, 1962, 1963, 1968, 1971, 1972, 1973, 1975, 1977, 1995 by The Lockman Foundation. Used by permission; the New King James Version (NKJV). Copyright © 1982 by Thomas Nelson, Inc. Used by permission. All rights reserved; and the *Holy Bible*, New Living Translation (NLT), copyright © 1996, 2004. Used by permission of Tyndale House Publishers, Inc., Wheaton, Illinois 60189. All rights reserved.

Printed in the United States of America

9 10 11 12 13 14 15 / 18 17 16 15 14

contents

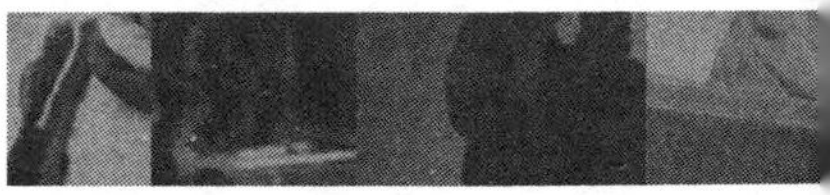

how to use this book

As I boarded the plane back to Oregon, I couldn't help but think, *If this church ends up looking like every other struggling church I've ever been in, what will we have accomplished?* On Sunday evenings, I had been flying to northern Idaho to meet with a small group of people who wanted to plant a new church and me to become their pastor. If I agreed, how could I ensure we did not end up like so many other churches: struggling to survive, hoping for a better way, but not reaching the potential of God's design for His church?

I accepted the offer to become their pastor, and the training manual you have in your hands explains how I and the rest of the leadership team at Real Life Ministries answered those questions. There isn't much theory here. Instead, it is the day-by-day, boots-on-the-ground game plan that we use every day at our church. For the next twelve weeks, I along with Avery Willis, Brandon Guindon, and Bill Krause will coach you through a clear and uncomplicated way to make disciples.

Avery is the executive director of the International Orality Network, and he speaks around the world to both oral and literate audiences. Brandon is the executive pastor at Real Life Ministries. He, along with his team, pioneered the small-groups ministry at Real Life. Bill serves as the family ministry team leader at Real Life Ministries. Together we have boiled down the lessons our church learned through trial and error and put them into this workbook format.

You will need twenty to thirty minutes five days each week to do the assignments. It is important for you to complete each learning exercise before reading further. Each day will include interactive activities, passages to look up, and a review section that will summarize what you should have learned. It is possible for you to work though this book on your own, but we recommend that you work through it with a group of three to ten people. If you are leading the group, we have a leader's guide at the back of this training manual that will help you facilitate the group.

By the end of the first week, you should be able to explain why making disciples is a priority for both you and your church. By the end of the twelfth week, you should be better equipped to make disciples. Our objective is that you will become a more intentional disciple-maker and have a strong grasp of the process Jesus modeled for us.

Jim Putman
Spring 2010

a heart to make disciples

The church in America is in decline. At the heart of this problem, good Christian people are lost as to what to do. These next twelve weeks are dedicated to what we believe will be a life-changing journey to restoring God's priorities to our lives. The church was built to win.

WHAT DOES WINNING LOOK LIKE?

day 1

When Jim Putman met with the people who wanted to plant a church in Idaho, it caused him to think about what a *successful* church would look like. Consequently, when he agreed to help start a new church, he asked the group he met with two questions: (1) If Christianity were a team sport and the church were Christ's team, what would winning be? (2) What is the church supposed to be and do to win?

Several people answered that the church wins as we worship together or when it grows in attendance and people become believers. A few said that we win when we are a family who cares for one another. Jim went on to ask what a church would have to do to accomplish all these goals. Some felt it would need inspiring weekend services with dynamic preaching and great music. Others thought the church should train people in pastoral care in order to meet the needs of hurting people.

1. Before you move ahead, write down your answers to these same questions.

   • In relation to Christianity and the church, what is winning?

   When the church members are making disciples —

   • What is the church supposed to be and do to win?

   be the body/presence of Christ — make disciples

The varying answers people gave caused Jim to turn to the Bible for a solution. The church needed a clear game plan or it would be divided from the start. Jesus' last command in Matthew 28:18-20 makes the church's mission clear: The church is called to reach the world for Jesus one person at a time. In other words, every Christian is commanded to participate in the mission to make disciples. This mission became Real Life Ministries' purpose.

That was ten years ago. Since then our church has grown to more than eight thousand people, and discipleship is happening in every ministry. Oh, we have made many mistakes and we still have a lot to learn, but God is leading and blessing our obedience to His command to make disciples.

Jesus came to them and said, "All authority in heaven and on earth has been given to me. Therefore go and make disciples of all nations, baptizing them in the name of the Father and of the Son and of the Holy Spirit, and teaching them to obey everything I have commanded you. And surely I am with you always, to the very end of the age."

(Matthew 28:18-20)

2. Read Matthew 28:18-20 in the margin and circle the words in which Jesus is telling us to do something.

   Did you circle the words *go*, *make disciples*, *baptizing*, and *teaching*?
   In the Bible's original language, *make disciples* is the key phrase in these verses because the words *going*, *baptizing*, and *teaching* support the command to make disciples.

3. In these verses, Jesus commanded us to go into the world and ___make___ ___disciples___ of every nation.

4. The three other action words show us what is entailed in obeying that command. To make disciples, we must be ___going___, ___baptizing___, and ___teaching___.

   Go back and review how you answered the two questions at the beginning of this lesson. Compare what you wrote with the command above.

5. Check the box below that fits best at this point:

   ☒ "Yes! I knew it. I am off to a good start because I knew that the church is supposed to make disciples."
   ☐ "No, I missed it. No one has ever explained the church's purpose to me like this before."
   ☐ "Well, I had it right, but I said it in a different way."
   ☐ "I disagree! I had a different answer, and I still think I am right."

   Your answers throughout this training manual will shape the discussions in your small group each week. Be sure not to skip over any of them. This process is designed to help you understand and remember the lesson.

6. In your own words, write what part the church plays in making disciples.
   ___provide training, atmosphere___

7. What is your personal role in helping the church make disciples?
   ___equipping___

8. Spend some time meditating on Matthew 28:18-20. Begin memorizing it phrase by phrase. You will be asked to write it from memory later. Using these verses, explain to someone today why the church should focus on making disciples. Write the name(s) of the person(s) you told or plan to tell. _____

_____

Review

- God designed the church to reach the world for Christ by making disciples.
- Making disciples was Jesus' original command.

day 2

HOW DO WE OBEY JESUS' COMMAND?

Yesterday we looked at Jesus' command to make disciples. Today we will take a closer look at the importance of making disciples in our homes, workplaces, and churches.

Jesus Completed His Work

During the Last Supper, before Jesus was arrested and taken to the cross, He prayed with His disciples. In His prayer, Jesus says, "I have brought you glory on earth by *completing the work you gave me to do*" (John 17:4, emphasis added). How could He say that He had completed the work God had given Him to do when He had not yet died on the cross and risen from the dead?

I have brought you glory on earth by completing the work you gave me to do. And now, Father, glorify me in your presence with the glory I had with you before the world began. I have revealed you to those whom you gave me out of the world. They were yours; you gave them to me and they have obeyed your word. Now they know that everything you have given me comes from you. For I gave them the words you gave me and they accepted them. They knew with certainty that I came from you, and they believed that you sent me. I pray for them. I am not praying for the world, but for those you have given me, for they are yours.

(John 17:4-9)

1. Read John 17:4-9 in the margin and underline the work Jesus had completed when He prayed this prayer.

The answer? In His prayer, Jesus said that He had completed the work of making disciples. The disciples were ready to go and make disciples themselves; all they needed was the Holy Spirit. If Jesus had died on the cross for our sins but had not made disciples who could deliver the message, none of us would have heard the good news. Jesus completed the message: He died for us and rose from the grave. He also created a way for people even today to hear that message: by releasing His disciples to go and make disciples, who in turn were released to go and make disciples, and so on.

2. Many people believe that Jesus came only to die and be resurrected from the dead. Why do you think they often leave out the work Jesus did of making disciples?

too hard

Look again in Matthew 28:18-20. A few weeks after His resurrection, Jesus commanded twelve men to do the same work His Father had given Him to do. The disciples didn't look at Jesus and say, "How do we do *that*?" Jesus had already shown them how; He had given them a living model to follow. Jesus made disciples who made other disciples.

3. What main work did Jesus say He had completed when He prayed to the Father in John 17? Circle the answer.

- Healed people who were sick
- Taught truth to the crowds
- Made twelve men into mature disciples
- Reformed Jewish worship
- Rose from the dead

The correct answer is the third one.

4. How can you know when your work with someone you are discipling is complete?

they are making disciples of others

The Message Needs a Messenger

Your work is complete when the person you are discipling can make a disciple. Some might question the need for disciples who can disciple others. After all, we have the Bible and the Holy Spirit. Aren't they enough to make disciples? We must remember that Jesus knew we would have both these things, yet He still told His disciples to go and to teach others to obey. Jesus knew that mature disciples were needed to deliver the message. Disciples are made when the Spirit of God, the Word of God, and the people of God work together.

5. Read Romans 10:14 in the margin and then rate the importance of a messenger. Circle your choice:

How, then, can they call on the one they have not believed in? And how can they believe in the one of whom they have not heard? And how can they hear without someone preaching to them?

(Romans 10:14)

(The messenger is essential.)   The messenger is very important.   The messenger is optional.   The messenger is unnecessary.

The church was not designed to be a group of spectators who attend weekly lectures; it was designed to be a trained army with a powerful message. *All* believers are the messengers who bring the message to others and then continue the process of discipling those who believe. By doing this, we complete the same work Jesus prayed about in John 17. He gave that work to His disciples, who in turn gave it to us.

How Are *We* Doing?

Statistics tell us that a typical believer will die without leading a single person to a life-saving relationship with Jesus Christ.[1] Before you say, "No way!" or "That figures!" ask yourself, *Who was the last person I led to Christ?*

According to Matthew 28:18-20, even if we have led someone to Christ, we need to ask another question. Have we discipled that person to the point that he or she is able to lead someone *else* to Christ and then disciple that new believer? We complete our work when our disciple can do his or her part to win and train new disciples who are then able to do the same with others. In this way, the process of making disciples continues until Jesus returns. His command to the church remains the same generation after generation.

6. Did you follow that? How can our work of making disciples be completed while the process of making disciples continues until Jesus returns? Write your answer using your own words.

As you consider your role in making disciples, spend time praying through Jesus' prayer in John 17.

7. Suppose someone challenges the belief that our first priority is to make disciples. Write how you would explain Jesus' example in John 17.

_____

_____

_____

_____

Review
- In John 17, Jesus prayed to the Father that He had completed the work He had been given.
- The work that Jesus had completed was training the twelve to be disciple-makers.
- God intended for the message of the gospel to come from a messenger who can disciple others.

MAKE DISCIPLES AS YOU GO

day 3

This is an important day. We are going to get even more practical about our role in what the church is supposed to do.

Evil Will Not Prevail

As a wrestler and a wrestling coach, Jim Putman knew the test of any athlete's ability was on the mat. Athletes may make bold claims, but the wrestling mat is where they back them up. Jesus made bold claims about his church.

1. Read Matthew 16:15-18 in the margin and underline the bold statement Jesus made about the church.

Jesus said that the gates of hell (or the forces of evil) would not prevail against (overcome or stop) His church from completing its mission. But it seems the church is being overcome all the time—there are divisions and splits, fights and feuds. Why aren't we seeing Jesus' words backed up on the mat? The church in America is not winning many converts, and it struggles to keep the ones it already has. So many indicators seem to say that the church is no match for the forces of evil. Should that be the case? No. Jesus meant what He said. So why aren't American Christians proving themselves "on the mat"?

He said to them, "But who do you say that I am?" Simon Peter replied, "You are the Christ, the Son of the living God." And Jesus answered him, "Blessed are you, Simon Bar-Jonah! For flesh and blood has not revealed this to you, but my Father who is in heaven. And I tell you, you are Peter, and on this rock I will build my church, and the <u>gates of hell shall not prevail against it.</u>"

(Matthew 16:15-18, ESV)

2. Take a minute and list the top three reasons you think the church is not winning many converts.

- Major in minors
- don't know how
- pass the buck to others

In his book *The Unchurched Next Door*, Thom Rainer cites a study that shows that most unchurched people do not sense that Christians actively try to share their faith and that many wonder what makes Christians hesitant.[2] In other words, many unchurched people would be open to talking about Christ, but Christians do not talk to them about their faith.

3. Why do you think a majority of unchurched people feel that Christians are reluctant to share their faith and, therefore, not advancing the kingdom?

4. Compare that with the roadblocks you listed previously. Were you off base?

5. What do you think it will take to turn the situation around so that evil is not prevailing against the church?

we go on the offensive —

A Real Life Ministries Story

Kelly owned the most popular Country Western bar in our town. He was a well-known performer in bars all over our area. He seemed very successful doing life without Jesus, but he knew something was missing. It was just a matter of time before he closed his bar. Through a variety of circumstances and relationships, Kelly accepted Christ, and some men in our church began to intentionally disciple him. Kelly began to share his life and heart with others as well. He now has a ministry in our church to help people do their finances God's way. He is still asked to perform all over the area, and at every performance he shares the gospel.

Kelly's story is a constant reminder to us that the church still works. It is able to take territory from the Enemy. Hell is no match for the power of Christ and His church.

"As You Are Going . . ."

The literal translation of the command in Matthew 28:19-20 is this: *"As you are going, make disciples!"* (emphasis added). Jesus is directing us to make disciples as we go about doing life. Matthew 16:15-18 reminds us that the Enemy has captured people and holds them from Christ. Disciple-makers are walking into a dark world that is in need of light.

6. What about you? As you read this, do you think about the non-Christians you know? Use the following categories to help you think of names of people who need Christ.

- Someone under your own roof
- Someone at work or school
- Someone you know because your kids play on the same team or have the same teacher
- Someone in your neighborhood or community
- A friend or family member

Pray for these folks this week. God is leading these people across your path. People we meet every day need Jesus, and the Enemy cannot stop us from sharing the gospel message with them. But disciple-making begins with our going to those who need to hear the message.

Here's an example of what we are talking about. One day on a whim, Jim Putman stopped by a local movie theater during off-hours to ask if the owners would rent space to our church. We were growing, and we needed more room. As he entered the waiting area, he saw an employee sitting there crying. Jim asked what was wrong, and her story spilled out. She and her husband had separated. As they talked about her struggles, Jim was able to share the message of salvation with her, and that morning she began her journey with

Jesus. God put this woman in Jim's path as he was going through his day. If Jim had ignored her problems and just asked about renting the theater, she would not have met Jesus that day. In the same way, when we see a person in need, it is an invitation from God to step in with love and service—and eventually with words—to point people to Christ.

7. As you go through your day, what is it that keeps you from making disciples?

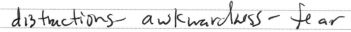

distractions awkwardness - fear

Review

- Jesus said that the forces of evil would not overcome His church.
- As we go along in life, we will meet people who need Jesus.

day 4

THE CHURCH IS GOD'S TEAM

Let's review . . .

1. In Matthew 28:18-20, Jesus commanded us to __make__ __disciples__.

2. In John 17, Jesus prayed to the Father about completing the work He had been given: making disciples. This work was important because the message of the gospel needs a __messenger__.

3. Yesterday, we embraced Jesus' claim that the forces of __hell__ will not __prevail__ against the __church__. The church is supposed to be a winning team that moves forward and crushes our Opponent's strongholds.

Make notes in the margins regarding what you would like to discuss in your small group about how the church should prevail. Invite God today to be part of your study.

Christianity Is a Team Sport

The church is God's team. Today some Christians think they can make disciples best without the church. They feel that the church (the corporate body) doesn't hold up its end. Because of this, they are sometimes tempted to quit the church and go the Christian life alone. But Christianity is a team sport. No matter how gifted or talented an individual is, he or she needs the church to be able to successfully make disciples and be a disciple. Because a "go it alone" philosophy is unbiblical. The church is part of God's design for disciple-making.

4. Read again Matthew 16:18: "I tell you, you are Peter, and on this rock I will build my church, and the gates of hell shall not prevail against it" (ESV). Jesus clearly tells us who is going to crush the gates of hell (the forces of evil). Check the one that is going to win the battle.

> ☐ Peter himself
> ☐ The twelve disciples
> ☑ The church

Sure, some parts of our faith can be accomplished on the individual level, but much of what the church is supposed to do can happen only when we function as a team. We can win (make disciples of all nations) only as a team.

5. The apostle Paul uses the human body to illustrate this principle. Read Romans 12:4-8 in the margin and write out how you think the church team functions like a body.

_____

_____

_____

_____

Just as each of us has one body with many members, and these members do not all have the same function, so in Christ we who are many form one body, and each member belongs to all the others. We have different gifts, according to the grace given us. If a man's gift is prophesying, let him use it in proportion to his faith. If it is serving, let him serve; if it is teaching, let him teach; if it is encouraging, let him encourage; if it is contributing to the needs of others, let him give generously; if it is leadership, let him govern diligently; if it is showing mercy, let him do it cheerfully.
(Romans 12:4-8)

The Bible makes it clear that although the church is made up of individuals, we must work together to succeed.

Follow Jesus, Not Me

The church team is also important because no one person has all the abilities, gifts, and wisdom of Jesus. We need each other to fulfill Christ's command. Though we are responsible to disciple those God brings across our paths, we were never intended to do it all alone. Working as a team helps us to keep Jesus first and avoid exalting one player's importance above another.

6. Think about the believers who surround you. Write down the name of someone you know who could:

• Help others locate Bible passages that shed light on a subject

_____

• Give empathy and encouragement when someone is struggling

_____

• Share wisdom about how God helped him or her work through marriage or parenting problems

_____

• Serve as a good host

_____

• Organize a service project

_____

In the church, people do all these things to cooperate with God in making disciples. There is still a need for a pastor, but he does not need to feel as if he must have all the wisdom, skills, or answers. The pastor can be real about his struggles because the solutions are not going to be found in him. You see, the pastor is not making disciples who follow *him*; he is making disciples who follow *Jesus*.

7. What abilities and gifts do you have that can help others be like Jesus?

_____

_____

_____

Paul told us in Ephesians 2:10 that we are God's masterpiece and that He saved us for good works that He planned for us to do. We all have roles we have been gifted and shaped to fulfill. Too many believers do not understand that even the scars we've received from others (and the ones we've given to ourselves) can be used now for Jesus.

A Real Life Ministries Story

Our church has a huge ministry to recovering addicts that meets in small groups. A team of people who were once alcoholics and drug addicts leads this ministry. The team members understand addiction because they have struggled with it for years. They have the experience with Jesus and know that He can save anyone out of anything. We also have groups for the sexually abused and the sexually addicted, led by folks who have found victory with Jesus in those areas. Everyone can be used in the church no matter what their past.

8. Earlier you wrote down your gifts and abilities that God might use to help others be like Jesus, but what about your scars? What has God brought you through that could be used to disciple others? *parenting issues —*
attitude toward illness
grief process

9. What areas of disciple-making could you use help?

Review

- Jesus called us to make disciples of Him, not ourselves.
- Every Christian has been given gifts to use for fulfilling Christ's command to go and make disciples.
- The church team offers a variety of gifts and abilities to make disciples together.

ON THIS TEAM, EVERYONE PLAYS

day 5

You made it! You are about to complete the first week. Be open to God's leading today.

Get in the Game

If Christianity is a team sport, then the team cannot win unless everyone gets in the game. Take a moment to read 1 Corinthians 12:14-20 in the margin.

Paul writes that we are *all* part of the church—God's team. We were chosen to be on this team and to play the role He gifted us for. We all have abilities and gifts to be used for the good of the team and the cause of Christ. Everyone is important and everyone plays.

Getting Started Can Be Hard

Scott attended one of our home groups. He listened intently each week to the discussion and quickly learned that it was okay to ask questions. People were drawn to Scott. His positive attitude and genuine enthusiasm were contagious. However, when Bill Krause asked him to consider leading a group, he hesitated. He was concerned that he did not know enough about the Bible to lead a group. He thought the leaders had to know Bible languages, understand ancient history, and so on.

Fear is one of the roadblocks that keep people from playing on the team. What if someone asks a question you cannot answer? None of us wants to look stupid. Others think they can't play on the team by leading a small group because they aren't a trained counselor, and still others say they are too busy and would be unable to do a good job. After all, time is not like money: We can't make more time.

The body is not made up of one part but of many. If the foot should say, "Because I am not a hand, I do not belong to the body," it would not for that reason cease to be part of the body. And if the ear should say, "Because I am not an eye, I do not belong to the body," it would not for that reason cease to be part of the body. If the whole body were an eye, where would the sense of hearing be? If the whole body were an ear, where would the sense of smell be? But in fact God has arranged the parts in the body, every one of them, just as he wanted them to be. If they were all one part, where would the body be? As it is, there are many parts, but one body.

(1 Corinthians 12:14-20)

1. What fears or concerns do you have about leading a discipleship group?

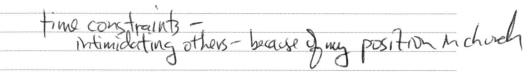

time constraints –
intimidating others – because of my position in church

Too often, fears and concerns paralyze people from ever playing on God's team. Worse yet, in some cases their concerns are excuses that hide an unwilling heart. They just don't want to get involved. Leading a discipleship group sounds like too much work.

Letting Others Play Can Be Harder Yet!

Jim Putman was having breakfast with a pastor from another church, and during their conversation, the pastor said he wondered why Real Life was growing while his was struggling. When Jim asked him if he was discipling his people, the pastor replied, "Absolutely!" He had been meeting with a small group of guys for a couple of hours every week for nearly two years.

Jim was puzzled. This pastor had been meeting with these folks for two years, yet he insisted that these disciples were not ready to be released. When we started our church, the need in our community was so great that we released people sooner than Jim was comfortable with, so he understood this pastor's desire to get it right. (To address this concern, we created a system so that people could get on-the-job training and accountability as they went.)

Jim pulled out a napkin and asked the pastor to write down everything a Christian needed to know in order to make disciples. He filled one side, then the other. Then he asked the waitress for another napkin. After filling it, he handed the napkins to Jim, who quickly saw the problem. The list of what a Christian must know in order to make disciples was the equivalent of what someone would know after graduating from seminary. This pastor believed that the people he discipled could not disciple others until they knew everything that he knew. He was seminary trained, so it would take a while.

2. What would have happened to the disciples if Jesus had thought like this pastor?

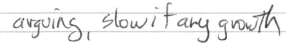

arguing, slow if any growth

Like Scott, Jeanne had fears about leading a small group. She was shy and had a reserved personality but believed God wanted her to get involved in women's ministry. Jeanne's small-group leader helped her get started by having her tell the story (see week 12) at her women's small group occasionally. As Jeanne's confidence grew, the women responded to her love of God's Word and commonsense approach to its application, and she eventually took over the leadership of the group. What Jeanne lacked in public-speaking confidence she made up for in caring for the women of her group. She was intentional about calling those who missed meetings and following up with those who were struggling. She made the time to be a good leader. She was willing to play on God's team, and she became a great player.

In the Game or in the Stands?

There are different vantage points from which to experience any game. Sadly, many Christians believe that the Christian life can be played from the stands. They never get on the field. In other words, they don't have a place of ministry and they don't share Christ with anyone. Instead, they watch their pastors and ministers play, as they are the paid professional players.

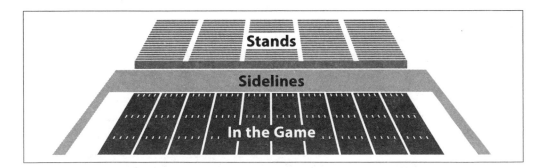

3. Put an "X" where you think you have been most of the last two years as a Christian who makes disciples. Have you been on the stands, on the sidelines, or in the game?

Stands   Sidelines   Game

4. Look again at this week's key verses, Matthew 28:18-20 (see day 1). Have you memorized it yet? How has your understanding of making disciples changed?

i know what needs to be done -- it's the doing that is hard

5. Has your commitment to making disciples grown? Mark the responses that best describe your commitment.

- ☑ I realize that I must be involved.
- ☐ I have always been committed.
- ☐ I've never thought much about it before.
- ☐ I am eager to make disciples.
- ☑ I am nervous.
- ☐ I need to be discipled myself.
- ☐ Other _____

6. Write what you will say to someone who asks, "Why should we be committed to making disciples?" *command found in Matt 28:18-20*

Be prepared to share your answers with your small group.

Review

- Disciple-making happens best when Christians play together as a team to make disciples.
- Each person has something to offer to disciple-making.
- We must get out of the stands and use our abilities "on the field" to make disciples.

what is a disciple?

This training manual can do only so much to coach you through discipleship. God will use the interactions in your small group to anchor these ideas and attitudes into your life. If you are not discussing your answers (and questions) with a group of people each week, ask some friends to join you in this study.

JESUS INVITES US TO BE DISCIPLES

1. So we can all get on the same page, please write your definition of a disciple. Don't move ahead until you do so!

A follower of Jesus who is growing and discipling others

Staff members from other churches often ask our leadership team for help, and we ask them the question we just asked you: What is your definition of a disciple? To this day, we have seen only one church whose staff had definitions that even came close to agreeing with each other. This is a serious problem! A disciple-making team must agree on what a disciple is.

A definition enables us to evaluate if we are disciples, and it helps others to understand what it means to be a disciple of Jesus. So at Real Life Ministries, we teach a biblical definition of discipleship that everyone in our church can remember. We believe that definition is found in Matthew 4:19: "Follow me, . . . and I will make you fishers of men."

2. In this chart, write in your own words the three parts of the definition of a disciple based on Jesus' invitation in Matthew 4:19.

Jesus' Words	Explaining Jesus' Words in My Words
"Follow me"	(1) A disciple . . . *obeys and lives for Jesus*
"I will make you"	(2) *allows God to make us the people he wants us to be*
"fishers of men"	(3) *disciples others*

Here is how we define *disciple* at Real Life Ministries: (1) A disciple knows and **follows** Christ; (2) a disciple is being **changed** by Christ; and (3) a disciple is committed to the **mission** of Christ. Go back and add the words in bold in the margin beside your definition.

"Follow Me"

The first part of this definition is an invitation to follow Jesus. If we follow Christ, we must come under His authority and direction. That is what *follow* means—someone else leads. Matthew 4:19 is an invitation to be in relationship with Jesus, but to be in that relationship, we must submit to His leadership.

3. Read the following statements and check the ones you agree with:

- ☐ I believe that Jesus is Savior and Lord.
- ☐ Following Him wholeheartedly frightens me.
- ☐ I obey Christ's commands.
- ☐ Trust is difficult for me, especially with God.
- ☐ I believe in Jesus, but I need to follow Him better as His disciple.

A disciple is someone who follows Jesus as Lord. Do you need to stop and talk to Him about how well you are doing as a disciple? If so, take a moment to do so now.

"I Will Make You"

The next part of the definition focuses on change. Jesus isn't a dead man or someone who left this world without a trace. He is alive, and He transforms us into new persons if we follow Him as His disciples. We are changed as we stay in relationship with Him through Bible study, prayer, the counsel of other believers, and life experiences.

Those God foreknew he also predestined to be conformed to the likeness of his Son, that he might be the firstborn among many brothers.

(Romans 8:29)

4. According to Romans 8:29 (in the margin), what are you being changed into?

Jesus

5. How has your relationship with Jesus changed you since you got serious about following Him?

A disciple is someone who is being changed by Jesus to be more like Him.

"Fishers of Men"

What did Jesus mean when He said that He was going to make the disciples into fishers of men? Peter's fishing crew had just brought in a humongous catch. The men must have thought, *Wow! We won't need to work for a few months after we sell all these fish!* This was a business they understood.

Read Luke 5:1-11 in the margin. This is Luke's account of the story.

Jesus seized this opportunity to begin the work He had come to complete: making disciples. He put disciple-making into a language these fishermen would understand. Fishers of men are those who work to fulfill Christ's command to make disciples of all nations.

6. Use the three parts of Jesus' words in Matthew 4:19 to complete the following chart.

Jesus' Invitation (Matthew 4:19)	A Disciple Is One Who . . .
	(1) Knows and follows Christ
	(2) Is being changed by Christ
	(3) Is committed to the mission of Christ

How Are You Doing?

When asked how they are doing with discipleship, many church leaders say something like this: "I make disciples every week. Three hundred people come to hear me preach God's Word every Sunday." Yet Jesus did not say in Matthew 4:19, "I am inviting you to be my disciples, so grab a pew and a pen. This week we're starting a four-part series on discipleship." We cannot change the definition of discipleship to (1) *sit* and (2) *listen*, and then expect to make disciples as Jesus did.

7. How well have your actions lined up with the Matthew 4:19 definition of discipleship? Check any that apply.

☑ My beliefs are accurate, but my follow-through is weak.
☐ I was never shown how to be a disciple.
☐ I think my beliefs and actions line up well.
☐ I have been confused in my definition of discipleship.

One day as Jesus was standing by the Lake of Gennesaret, with the people crowding around him and listening to the word of God, he saw at the water's edge two boats, left there by the fishermen, who were washing their nets. He got into one of the boats, the one belonging to Simon, and asked him to put out a little from shore. Then he sat down and taught the people from the boat.

When he had finished speaking, he said to Simon, "Put out into deep water, and let down the nets for a catch."

Simon answered, "Master, we've worked hard all night and haven't caught anything. But because you say so, I will let down the nets."

When they had done so, they caught such a large number of fish that their nets began to break. So they signaled their partners in the other boat to come and help them, and they came and filled both boats so full that they began to sink.

When Simon Peter saw this, he fell at Jesus' knees and said, "Go away from me, Lord; I am a sinful man!" For he and all his companions were astonished at the catch of fish they had taken, and so were James and John, the sons of Zebedee, Simon's partners.

Then Jesus said to Simon, "Don't be afraid; from now on you will catch men." So they pulled their boats up on shore, left everything and followed him.

(Luke 5:1-11)

8. Go back and read Luke 5:1-11 again. What are you avoiding doing that you know needs to be done in order to follow Jesus more completely? Write down what comes to mind in the space below, and pray about sharing it in your small group.

Review

- Christians are confused about the definition of a disciple, which is a roadblock to making disciples together.
- A disciple is defined in Matthew 4:19 as one who follows Jesus, is being changed by Jesus, and is on mission with Him.

"FOLLOW ME"

day 2

A clear definition of *disciple* cuts two ways. The first part of the definition challenges us to assess our own commitment. The second helps us disciple others. This week we're focused on our personal commitment to discipleship so that later we can help others grow.

The Invitation to Follow

Peter believed that Jesus was the Messiah, and his actions backed up his beliefs. To follow means to acknowledge Jesus in His entirety. Yes, He is Savior, but He also said that to follow Him meant to obey Him (see John 14:23-24).

1. Read John 12:26 in the margin. What is Jesus saying in this verse about His position in the discipleship process? *leader*

_____

_____

_____

_____

_____

_____

_____

_____

_____

_____

Anyone who wants to be my disciple must follow me, because my servants must be where I am. And the Father will honor anyone who serves me.
(John 12:26, NLT)

The point Jesus made over and again is that to be one of His disciples, we must follow Him. "I will lead," Jesus says. "You will go where I want you to go. You will do what I want you to do." When we surrender to Jesus as Savior, He expects to be Lord. In Matthew 4:19, His invitation made it clear that He would be the leader. Take it or leave it. We begin to be disciples when we understand that we are positioned *behind* Jesus. He leads. We follow.

2. List five characteristics that you desire in someone you are going to follow:

- *integrity*
- *consistency*
- _____
- _____
- _____

Look over your list. Are not all of these characteristics of Jesus Christ? Take a few minutes to ask in prayer if your current commitment is the same as your initial commitment to follow Jesus as Savior and Lord. Is Jesus asking you to make a deeper commitment? Listen to your Lord.

Once again, we come to the first part of our definition: A disciple is one who follows Christ. Disciples are affected at the head level—we *acknowledge* Jesus as Lord—and we follow Jesus as our head. This is what it means to believe.

We can picture the first part of the definition this way:

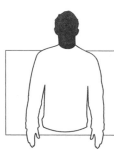

Discipleship involves a head-level change:
A disciple knows who Christ is and makes a decision to follow Him.

This head-level change is the first step, but as we will see throughout this week, there's much more to this definition. Following Jesus leads to changes in our motives and actions, as we will see.

How About You?

Accepting Jesus' invitation to follow Him begins with realizing who He is. Following Jesus affects the disciple's thinking. This head-level change challenges everything from our worldview to our priorities. Peter, James, and John believed that Jesus was the Messiah. They were so convinced that they took a drastic step: They left everything to answer His call to follow Him. Are you convinced? Have you come to the place that you believe that Jesus is who He said He was? That God actually proved who Jesus was by resurrecting Him from the dead? If you haven't, you are still on the fence about following Him.

3. Have you made the decision that Jesus is both your Savior and Lord and that you will follow Him?

 ☐ Yes, most definitely.
 ☐ Yes, but I am afraid of the unknown.
 ☐ I am still not sure.
 ☐ No, I am not convinced.
 ☐ I just don't want to right now.

If you checked "Yes, most definitely," you are a disciple of Jesus. If you checked "Yes, but I am afraid," that is okay. Following Christ can take us through uncharted areas at times, but Jesus is with us. If you checked any of the other boxes, you must take action to either find answers to your questions or come to grips with the fact that you might not be Jesus' disciple.

Leaving Things Behind

For these fishermen, following Jesus meant leaving some things behind.

4. Read Luke 9:23-24 in the margin. In the chart, write what Jesus is calling His disciples to leave in order to follow Him and what He is telling them to pick up.

What Jesus Is Calling Them to Leave	What Jesus Is Telling Them to Pick Up
possessions priorities	*cross*

Then he said to them all: "If anyone would come after me, he must deny himself and take up his cross daily and follow me. For whoever wants to save his life will lose it, but whoever loses his life for me will save it. What good is it for a man to gain the whole world, and yet lose or forfeit his very self? If anyone is ashamed of me and my words, the Son of Man will be ashamed of him when he comes in his glory and in the glory of the Father and of the holy angels."

(Luke 9:23-24)

In the column on the left, you could have answers such as "self," "life lived their way," "thinking like people," "worldly gain," "fear of being ridiculed for believing in Jesus." On the right you should have answers such as "taking up their crosses," "following Jesus," "losing their lives for Jesus," "an eternal perspective."

What stands in the way of you following Jesus? If you cannot bring everything in your life under His authority, such as media or an ungodly relationship, you must abandon those things. This does not mean that you must leave your home and loved ones in order to follow Jesus. Followers of Jesus have families, jobs, and homes, but they follow Him all the same. For most of us, the big-ticket item we need to leave behind is self. In other words, following Jesus means we have to leave our selfish ambitions and our selfish way of life. Jesus said that we must take up our crosses daily and die to self (see Luke 9:23).

5. In the chart write some things Jesus is asking you to leave or pick up so you can follow Him as Lord.

What Jesus Is Calling Me to Leave	What Jesus Is Telling Me to Pick Up

How will you follow through with what you have written? Here is a suggestion. This week ask your small group to help you daily leave behind what Jesus is calling you to leave and to pick up the right things. See what advice or encouragement the group can give to help you.

Review

- Discipleship involves a head-level change. A disciple knows who Christ is and makes a decision to follow Him.
- Following Jesus means that everything has been brought under His authority. He is both Savior and Lord.

"AND I WILL MAKE YOU"

day 3

We hope this training manual and your regular interactions with the Lord are establishing a rhythm in your life. If you are struggling to get the assignments finished, make choices to clear time and find a quiet place. Keep the rhythm going.

A Disciple's Growth and Change

Jesus made it clear that He intended to change those who follow Him. His words "I will make you" indicated that God has a plan and the ability to change us. A disciple begins with a head-level change: He or she makes a decision to follow Christ. But *knowing* who Jesus is is just the first part of the definition. To be a disciple means that what we know is moving to our heart. What we know causes change in our character.

A disciple is one who is being changed by Jesus. He is making us into someone different. He changes hearts, which means our attitudes and priorities begin to shift. This kind of change is supernatural and is evidenced by a love for God and for others. The Holy Spirit is making us into relational people with an eternal perspective. God intends to use these relationships to lead a broken world to the transforming power of Jesus. His power makes these relationships possible.

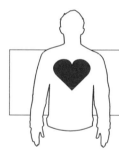

Discipleship involves a heart-level change:
A disciple is being changed by Christ.

1. Meditate on Romans 12:1-2 (in the margin) and write out a prayer here asking God to change you in the places and ways He brings to mind.

Lord, help me make decisions that honor you —

In Acts 3 and 4, Peter and John are on trial for preaching in public about Jesus. Earlier that day, God used them to heal a lame man. The next morning, they were brought to trial for the public disruption they had caused. Peter and John were not just fishermen from Galilee anymore.

2. Read Acts 4:13 in the margin. What brought about change in Peter and John?

They had been w/ Jesus

I urge you, brothers, in view of God's mercy, to offer your bodies as living sacrifices, holy and pleasing to God—this is your spiritual act of worship. Do not conform any longer to the pattern of this world, but be transformed by the renewing of your mind. Then you will be able to test and approve what God's will is—his good, pleasing and perfect will.
(Romans 12:1-2)

When they saw the courage of Peter and John and realized that they were unschooled, ordinary men, they were astonished and they took note that these men had been with Jesus.

(Acts 4:13)

Being with Jesus transformed Peter and John into world changers who cared about the plight of a beggar and who boldly preached about Jesus. When Jesus called them to follow Him, He saw potential that neither they nor anyone else saw. As they followed Him, they spent time with Him and He changed them.

Peter and John were not changed instantly into the courageous men who testified before the court. That encourages all of us. Jesus changes us (1) through a relationship, and (2) over time. He uses many different things to bring about this change, but the key ingredient is being with Him. As we spend time with Him, Jesus makes us more and more like Him in our inner persons, our hearts, and our characters (see 2 Corinthians 3:18).

I am the vine; you are the branches. If a man remains in me and I in him, he will bear much fruit; apart from me you can do nothing.

(John 15:5)

3. Read John 15:5 in the margin, and list some ways you can spend time connecting with Jesus.

prayer, bible study, serving

Did your list include things such as praying, reading the Bible, memorizing Scripture, and spending time with other Christians? More ways to consciously spend time personally with Christ include writing in a prayer journal, reading books by Christian authors, and listening to Bible teaching.

How About You?

Jesus changes us through the ways mentioned above. We get to know Him more and receive His direction and guidance about how to live.

I pray that out of his glorious riches he may strengthen you with power through his Spirit in your inner being, so that Christ may dwell in your hearts through faith. And I pray that you, being rooted and established in love, may have power, together with all the saints, to grasp how wide and long and high and deep is the love of Christ, and to know this love that surpasses knowledge—that you may be filled to the measure of all the fullness of God.

(Ephesians 3:16-19)

4. Read Ephesians 3:16-19 in the margin. Circle the words that show where the change takes place. Draw a box around the phrase that refers to Jesus being with us. Underline the words and phrases that describe the results of being with Jesus.

You should have circled *inner being* and drawn a box around *dwell in your hearts through faith*. As a result of Christ changing our characters, our hearts are filled with love for Him and for others. You should have underlined the word *love* three times, and you could have underlined other phrases such as *rooted and established in love, grasp how wide and long and high and deep is the love of Christ*, and *know this love that surpasses knowledge*.

5. Go back to your list of ways to spend time with Jesus. Choose three that you think are most important and write them in the left-hand column of this chart. In the column on the right, circle the most accurate description of your behavior.

Way to Spend Time with Jesus	How Frequently Do I Spend Time This Way?
1.	Daily 3–5 times a week Once a week A couple times a month Rarely, if ever
2.	Daily 3–5 times a week Once a week A couple times a month Rarely, if ever
3.	Daily 3–5 times a week Once a week A couple times a month Rarely, if ever

6. Start with the activity you do most frequently. Write one way you could encourage yourself to do this activity more often so that you continue to grow.

_____

_____

_____

_____

7. Next take the one you are weakest in doing. Write one way you could go to the next level of frequency in your weekly routine.

_____

_____

_____

8. If you can, write Matthew 4:19 from memory. If you can't, look it up and copy it here.

_____

_____

_____

Review

- Disciples experience a heart-level change by being with Christ.
- Having a relationship with Jesus requires that we spend time with Him, and as we spend time with Him, He changes us.

day 4

"FISHERS OF MEN"

A disciple makes a serious commitment to follow Jesus. Today's lesson is not meant to discourage or overwhelm you, but it might. Throughout this lesson, keep reminding yourself of Paul's words from Philippians 4:13, "I can do everything through him who gives me strength."

A Real Life Ministries Story

Bill Krause got a call last week from Scott, the new small-group leader you read about earlier. He said that he had a friend at work who was having some big problems and that he'd come alongside to help. Scott talked with his friend about his own faith in Jesus, and now his friend was ready to become a Christian. Scott was so excited; he called Bill to share his good news.

Scott sees the world in a different way, and he is joining the battle for the souls of men and women. He is a father of five and a small-business owner. He is a busy guy; however, he is finding time for the mission of Christ. Following Jesus has changed Scott's life.

What Was Jesus' Mission?

The mission of Jesus is seen and stated clearly during His encounter with Zacchaeus (read Luke 19:1-10 in the margin). Over dinner, Zacchaeus put his faith in Jesus as the Messiah. Jesus proclaimed publicly that Zacchaeus was saved; that day the kingdom of God had come to his home.

Jesus entered Jericho and was passing through. A man was there by the name of Zacchaeus; he was a chief tax collector and was wealthy. He wanted to see who Jesus was, but being a short man he could not, because of the crowd. So he ran ahead and climbed a sycamore-fig tree to see him, since Jesus was coming that way.

When Jesus reached the spot, he looked up and said to him, "Zacchaeus, come down immediately. I must stay at your house today." So he came down at once and welcomed him gladly.

All the people saw this and began to mutter, "He has gone to be the guest of a 'sinner.'"

But Zacchaeus stood up and said to the Lord, "Look, Lord! Here and now I give half of my possessions to the poor, and if I have cheated anybody out of anything, I will pay back four times the amount."

Jesus said to him, "Today salvation has come to this house, because this man, too, is a son of Abraham. For the Son of Man came to seek and to save what was lost."

(Luke 19:1-10)

1. In the middle of this dinner, Jesus stated His mission clearly (see Luke 19:10). What did He say that He had come to do?

seek : save lost people

2. Compare Jesus' words in Matthew 4:19 to His words in Luke 19:10. Circle the phrases in these two verses that are related to the mission of Jesus Christ.

Matthew 4:19 — "Follow me, and I will make you fishers of men."

Luke 19:10 — "For the Son of Man came to seek and to save what was lost."

"Fishers of men" and "to seek and to save what was lost" both speak to the mission of Christ. Disciples join Jesus in His mission. Jesus broadened the concept of "fishers of men" when He challenged Peter after he had denied Jesus.

3. Read John 21:15-19 in the margin and state how Jesus further defined Peter's role.

_____

_____

_____

Here Jesus let Peter know that taking care of the sheep was also his responsibility. We have already studied Jesus' last command to the disciples, in which He summed up His instructions to them (see Matthew 28:18-20).

4. Read Matthew 28:18-20 in the margin. Jesus' final command is His mission. In your own words, write His mission as stated in the passage.

_____

_____

_____

Becoming a fisher of men means we also become shepherds of His sheep. Making disciples means caring for Jesus' flock.

A Disciple's Hands

When we know Christ, we start to look at people differently. As we spend time with Jesus as our head (our "boss"), we begin to have a change of heart that leads to a change in how we use our hands. We want to serve God wherever He has placed us. This means that our abilities, gifts, and learned skills are all empowered and on call for the Lord's mission of making disciples of all nations.

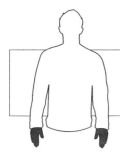

Discipleship involves a hands-level change:
A disciple is committed to the mission of Christ.

A Big Task

You may wonder, _But there are so many people with so many needs, and I am limited; where do I start?_ The beauty of God's plan is that we do not do the work of discipleship alone. Remember?

Erica is a coach over two other small-group leaders. How did she get to that place? Beth, another small-group leader shared the gospel with her a few years ago. For two years, Erica came to a small group. She asked questions about the Bible and Christian living week after week. As she read the Bible, learned to pray, and listened to God's Word being preached, she continued to grow. Then Erica was asked to lead a small group. She was excited to be asked but didn't think she could do it, yet Beth and others came alongside her and showed her how. Every week Erica had new questions about leading, and

When they had finished eating, Jesus said to Simon Peter, "Simon son of John, do you truly love me more than these?"

"Yes, Lord," he said, "you know that I love you."

Jesus said, "Feed my lambs."

Again Jesus said, "Simon son of John, do you truly love me?"

He answered, "Yes, Lord, you know that I love you."

Jesus said, "Take care of my sheep."

The third time he said to him, "Simon son of John, do you love me?"

Peter was hurt because Jesus asked him the third time, "Do you love me?" He said, "Lord, you know all things; you know that I love you."

Jesus said, "Feed my sheep. I tell you the truth, when you were younger you dressed yourself and went where you wanted; but when you are old you will stretch out your hands, and someone else will dress you and lead you where you do not want to go." Jesus said this to indicate the kind of death by which Peter would glorify God. Then he said to him, "Follow me!"

(John 21:15-19)

Jesus came to them and said, "All authority in heaven and on earth has been given to me. Therefore go and make disciples of all nations, baptizing them in the name of the Father and of the Son and of the Holy Spirit, and teaching them to obey everything I have commanded you. And surely I am with you always, to the very end of the age."

(Matthew 28:18-20)

every week she found answers through a phone call, a training time, or a conversation with another leader. Erica was part of a team. Now she has come alongside two small-group leaders and is helping them become disciple-makers as part of a team.

Erica is following Jesus (head), being changed by Jesus (heart), and is actively involved (hands) with Jesus' mission. She is doing the work Jesus commanded: She is making disciples.

Erica is not alone. She is part of our church team here at Real Life, and many people are helping her obey Jesus' command to make disciples. This relational discipleship process goes both ways, as there are several people helping Erica and several whom Erica is helping as well. Jesus never intended, nor does He want, any of us to go it alone. His design is making disciples together. Church really is a team sport. His mission is best accomplished when we do it together.

5. Below are some "hands-on" applications of the mission of Jesus. Place a check by the ones that you do and an "X" by the ones you want to work on doing.

☐ Attend community activities to meet non-Christians

☐ Participate in Little League and meet non-Christians

☐ Serve at a local soup kitchen or rescue mission

☐ Invite unchurched neighbors over to my house for a meal or game night

☐ Invite non-Christian acquaintances to concerts and events at my church

☐ Help with a church-sponsored harvest party

☐ Serve at a nursing home or retirement center

☐ Serve on community committees and meet non-Christians

☐ Offer Christian books or resources to people I know

6. List some other ways that you could be on mission with Jesus.

_____

_____

_____

_____

Be prepared to discuss your answers in the small-group session.

Review
- Discipleship involves a hands-level change. A disciple is committed to the mission of Christ.
- We are not to do this by ourselves. The church is God's team to make disciples.

THE INVITATION IS THE DEFINITION!

day 5

You are off to a solid start and are about to complete week 2. Your consistency indicates your commitment to completing this process. Congratulate yourself and the others in your group and keep going.

The Definition of a Disciple

All week we have been learning that Jesus' invitation encompasses the definition of a disciple:

"Follow me, . . . and I will make you fishers of men."

When someone comes to know who Jesus is and follows Him, it requires a head-level commitment. Following Jesus requires a decision to allow Him to be the authority (leader or head), which begins to change a disciple's way of thinking and seeing the world. Soon what a disciple knows begins to affect his or her attitudes and priorities. It begins to reflect the supernatural change of the Holy Spirit at work; this is a heart-level change. Last but not least, a commitment to the mission of Christ grows in a disciple, and the disciple aligns his or her efforts and resources with the mission of Jesus. When Christ's mission affects how a disciple lives, change is happening at the hands-level.

1. Please fill in the blanks with the words from this box:

mission	committed
following	changed

- A disciple is one who is _____*following*_____ Jesus. (head-level change)
- A disciple is one who is being _____*changed*_____ by Jesus. (heart-level change)
- A disciple is one who is _____*committed*_____ to the _____*mission*_____ of Jesus. (hands-level change)

Matthew 4:19 gives us a clear definition of a disciple that can be useful in several ways. A clear definition of a disciple can act as a measuring stick for our own spiritual maturity. It can also give new Christians a clear destination. Are they followers of Jesus? Have they entered into a relationship with Him to be changed by Him? Are they increasingly dedicating their time and energy to His mission? A clear definition of a disciple also helps us be on the same page with the church team so that we can walk with them intentionally as they grow and mature.

Because we are at the end of this week, take a moment to look deeper at your life as a disciple in light of the definition. As you answer the following questions, keep your weekly schedule (time) and your monthly budget (money) in mind.

2. Reflect on your life as a disciple. For each exercise, place an "X" above the description that best describes you right now. (Remember, we are just starting this journey and will help one another as we grow.)

1. **"Follow me"** — Am I someone who follows Jesus?

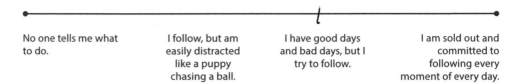

| No one tells me what to do. | I follow, but am easily distracted like a puppy chasing a ball. | I have good days and bad days, but I try to follow. | I am sold out and committed to following every moment of every day. |

2. **"And I will make you"** — Is Jesus changing me?

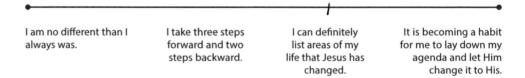

| I am no different than I always was. | I take three steps forward and two steps backward. | I can definitely list areas of my life that Jesus has changed. | It is becoming a habit for me to lay down my agenda and let Him change it to His. |

3. **"Fishers of men"** — At what level is my commitment to the mission of Jesus?

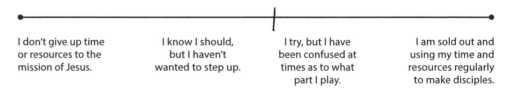

| I don't give up time or resources to the mission of Jesus. | I know I should, but I haven't wanted to step up. | I try, but I have been confused at times as to what part I play. | I am sold out and using my time and resources regularly to make disciples. |

Share your answers this week in your small group. Allow the group to affirm your strengths and give suggestions about how you might view yourself more accurately as a disciple of Jesus.

3. Review the definition of a disciple. What aspect of this definition do you need to grow in most? Write one action that you could take by tomorrow evening that would move you ahead in this area.

_____

_____

_____

A Relationship

Before we leave our discussion of the definition of a disciple, we need to note that Jesus called His disciples to join with Him. He was not inviting them to attend a class or listen to weekly lectures. He did not sit on a throne and demand tribute from them. Jesus invited His disciples to be in relationship with Him. They traveled together. They ate together. At times He spoke to them as a teacher, and other times He talked with them as a brother, but He was not just another buddy or acquaintance. Jesus is the Son of God. He is almighty God in the flesh of humanity. In John 15:14, Jesus says an amazing thing: "You are my friends if you do what I command." Be careful not to brush over His words. The God of the universe, our Creator and Lord, calls His disciples *friends*. God is our ruler, sovereign, a designer, and the builder of all heaven and earth—and He is our friend. He desires a relationship with you.

4. Take time to pray about what God is telling you. Write out some specifics that you want prayer for to help you follow Jesus.

5. Write Matthew 4:19 from memory.

Follow me and I will make you fishes of men.

6. Write the three parts of the definition of a disciple from Matthew 4:19.

- one who follows Jesus

- one who is growing - into the image of Christ

- one who disciples others

Review
- The definition of disciple from Matthew 4:19 includes change at the head-level, the heart-level, and the hands-level.
- The definition helps us evaluate our own growth, and it helps us show others a clear path to growing as a disciple.

how disciples grow

This week we shift gears. When everyone in the church understands Christ's command (see week 1) and has a clear definition of a disciple (see week 2), they can work together as God's team to go and make disciples. When we understand how a disciple grows, we begin to see how we can be intentional to make disciples.

By the end of this week, you will be able to name the stages of growth for a disciple, understand the basic characteristics and needs of each stage, and recognize some key phrases that people say in each stage. This week will also help you assess your own spiritual maturity. As you begin each day, ask God for insight and understanding.

THE SPIRITUALLY DEAD

day 1

What if you had never heard the gospel? Where do you think you would be if you were ignorant of God's desire to have a relationship with you? The Bible teaches that we were all spiritually dead and separated from God until we received grace through believing in Christ.

1. Read Ephesians 2:1-5 in the margin. Underline the phrase that says we were dead. Put a checkmark for the situations you have personally experienced that were evidences of spiritual death.

☑ Living in "your transgressions and sins"
☑ Following "the ways of this world"
☑ Following "the spirit who is now at work in those who are disobedient"
☐ "Gratifying the cravings of [your] sinful nature"
☑ "Following [the] desires and thoughts" of your sinful nature

Be prepared to discuss your answers in the small-group session.

Characteristics of the Spiritually Dead

People will reveal their spiritual condition (see Matthew 7:17; 12:34). Two words that best characterize those who are spiritually dead are *unbelief* and *rebellion*. They might shake their fist at God or be angry at some hurt or injustice that they blame on Him. Perhaps they refuse to have anyone (including God) tell them what to do. Some may *say* that they are not against God, but their lifestyle reveals a heart of rebellion. Ignoring Him always results in spiritual death.

We should not be surprised when spiritually dead people act in unbelief, rebellion, and rejection of God's will. They are acting according to their human nature and cannot change until they have been made alive in Christ. Spiritually dead people are deceived

As for you, you were dead in your transgressions and sins, in which you used to live when you followed the ways of this world and of the ruler of the kingdom of the air, the spirit who is now at work in those who are disobedient. All of us also lived among them at one time, gratifying the cravings of our sinful nature and following its desires and thoughts. Like the rest, we were by nature objects of wrath. But because of his great love for us, God, who is rich in mercy, made us alive with Christ even when we were dead in transgressions—it is by grace you have been saved.

(Ephesians 2:1-5)

(see John 8:44), and though they might threaten and ridicule the Christian faith, they are blind to the truth. They may not even realize it, but they are in desperate need of a Savior. The only Savior that can help them is Jesus Christ. Becoming His disciple is their only hope.

Pray also for me, that whenever I open my mouth, words may be given me so that I will fearlessly make known the mystery of the gospel, for which I am an ambassador in chains. Pray that I may declare it fearlessly, as I should.
(Ephesians 6:19-20)

2. What does Paul's request in Ephesians 6:19-20 (in the margin) say to you about any fear or hesitation you have in interacting with people who are spiritually dead?

Pray for strength —

"The Phrase from the Stage"

Our words and actions reveal where we are in the spiritual growth process. At Real Life Ministries we teach disciple-makers to intentionally listen for what we call "the phrase from the stage." These phrases help us assess spiritual growth—both ours and those we are discipling.

3. Here are some typical phrases the spiritually dead say. Check the ones you have heard.

- ☐ "I don't believe there is a God."
- ☐ "The Bible is just a bunch of myths."
- ☐ "God is just a crutch."
- ☑ "I am not a Christian because religion is responsible for most of the wars in history."
- ☐ "There are many ways to get to God."
- ☐ "There is no hell because God is a God of love."
- ☐ "I have been a good person, so I will be okay."
- ☐ "There is no absolute right and wrong."
- ☐ "I'll take my chances with the man upstairs."

4. Select one phrase that you checked, and write how you might begin a spiritual conversation with someone who says that phrase.

Xpianty is not a religion - it's a relationship

The Spiritually Dead's Needs

The spiritually dead need:

- An explanation of the gospel
- To see the gospel lived out
- Answers to their questions about the Bible, God, Christianity, and so on
- An invitation to receive Christ

5. In week 1, you wrote the names of family, friends, and acquaintances that are spiritually dead. Pray that God will help you meet the above spiritual needs in each person you identified.

Review

- Everyone starts out spiritually dead.
- The spiritually dead are characterized by unbelief and rebellion.
- Listening to people helps us identify what stage they are in. This is referred to as "the phrase from the stage."

day 2   THE SPIRITUAL INFANT

One of Jesus' most profound sayings is "No one can see the kingdom of God unless he is born again" (John 3:3). Becoming a Christian is a new beginning. When a person accepts Jesus as Savior and Lord, he or she passes from spiritual death to life and is born again as a spiritual infant. The process of becoming more like Jesus has just begun.

Some spiritual infants have been Christians for a long time but are stuck in this stage. They never grew up spiritually after they were saved. Attending church and carrying a Bible is all they know of the Christian life. Disciple-makers cooperate with God to help these infants grow.

Characteristics of Spiritual Infants

The words that best characterize this stage of a disciple's life are *ignorance*, *confusion*, and *dependence*.

1. Why do you think each of the following is true of spiritual infants?

    *   Ignorance *infants don't know what is important*

    *   Confusion *infants don't have a good sense of direction*

    *   Dependence *infants will not survive w/out a caregiver*

Consider these answers: Ignorance, because spiritual infants don't know much about biblical truth. They may mix a little of several religions and cultural beliefs with Christianity because they don't know any better. Confusion, because they don't know how to replace old, familiar habits with the habits and attitudes of a disciple. Dependence, because they cannot accomplish growth alone any more than a baby can feed and care for itself the day it comes home from the hospital.

Regardless of our physical age, when we first become believers, we are spiritual babies. We may have degrees from colleges and universities, but each one of us enters the Christian life as an infant. We may be Fortune 500 executives, but that does not allow us to skip the period where we are learning about Christ and the Bible for the first time.

"The Phrase from the Stage"

When people are spiritual infants, their words and their actions reveal it.

2. Here are some typical phrases a spiritual infant might say. Check the ones you have heard.

☐ "Why do I need to go to church regularly?"
☐ "I've been hurt by a lot of people, so it's just me and God. I don't need others."
☐ "I don't need anyone else, just me and Jesus."
☐ "If I pray and read my Bible, will I be good enough?"
☐ "I provide for my family. I don't have time for the church."
☐ "What should I do about my old friends who don't believe?"
☐ "I didn't know the Bible said that."
☐ "I know that Jesus is Lord and Savior, but is karma real?"
☐ "Does God let dead people, such as my grandma, visit us to give us messages from Him?"

A Spiritual Infant's Needs

Both physical babies and spiritual infants need someone to care for and feed them in order for them to grow and thrive.

3. Read 1 Peter 2:2-3 in the margin and underline what newborn spiritual babies need in order to grow.

> *As newborn babes, desire the <u>pure milk of the word</u>, that you may grow thereby, if indeed you have tasted that the Lord is gracious.*
> *(1 Peter 2:2-3, NKJV)*

You should have underlined *the pure milk of the word.*

Paul gave us a model in 1 Thessalonians 2:6-8 for meeting the spiritual needs of infants. Some of their critical needs are:

*   The personal attention of a disciple-maker/spiritual parent
*   Care and protection during this vulnerable stage of discipleship
*   Teaching and modeling the new truths of the Christian faith
*   Developing new habits that become the rhythms they will live by as disciples

4. With Paul's attitude from 1 Thessalonians 2:6-8 in mind, what are some things a disciple-maker can do to help meet these needs?

gentleness, love, nurture, non-judgmental

> *We were not looking for praise from men, not from you or anyone else. As apostles of Christ we could have been a burden to you, but we were gentle among you, like a mother caring for her little children. We loved you so much that we were delighted to share with you not only the gospel of God but our lives as well, because you had become so dear to us.*
> *(1 Thessalonians 2:6-8)*

5. Read the following list of new habits that spiritual infants need to learn and place a checkmark beside any that you may need to develop in yourself.

☐ Weekly church attendance   ☐ Tithing   ☑ Discerning media intake
☑ Regular Bible reading   ☑ Putting off sin   ☑ Avoiding temptation
☑ Having a prayer life   ☑ Forgiving others   ☑ Redirecting thought life
☑ Sharing their faith   ☑ Serving others   ☑ Weekly discipleship meeting

It is important that spiritual infants see mature believers (disciple-makers) living the discipleship lifestyle so that they can imitate these behaviors.

This does not mean that disciple-makers are perfect. Spiritual infants also need to watch how mature Christians deal with failure and mistakes. God uses a variety of people to teach and help spiritual infants grow. However, a spiritual infant typically requires an intentional investment from a disciple-maker/spiritual parent.

6. Write the names of any spiritual infants you know and ask God what they need to grow. Commit to more intentionally leading the spiritual babies that God brings to you to disciple.

_____
_____
_____
_____
_____
_____

Review

- The second stage of spiritual growth is infancy.
- Spiritual infants are characterized by ignorance, confusion, and dependency.
- Physical age, education, and life experiences do not exempt anyone from entering the Christian life as an infant.
- Spiritual infants need individual attention to thrive.

THE SPIRITUAL CHILD

day 3

While it is helpful to know what a mature disciple looks and acts like, don't fall into the trap of comparing levels of spiritual maturity. Speaking in such terms is a sure sign of spiritual immaturity!

Another caution: Don't mistake Bible knowledge, years of church attendance, physical age, education, and so forth for spiritual maturity. A person's *physical* maturity is easy to identify. Not so with a person's *spiritual* maturity. Some spiritually **immature** people have been in church for sixty years or more. And some spiritually **mature** disciples have been Christians for only a few years.

The apostle Paul almost always used the language of family when he wrote about discipleship. He was a spiritual parent to many, and when he wrote to them in his letters, he addressed them as his children in the faith.

1. Read the passages from the New Testament in the margin. Copy words from these Scriptures that describe the growth stage or the relationship between a disciple-maker and the growing disciple.

Passage	Defining or Describing Spiritual Childhood
1 Thessalonians 2:10-12	children
1 Timothy 1:1-2	son
Philemon 1:8-11	son

The above verses make it clear that Paul, as a disciple-maker, intentionally invested in people who had been born again into the life of a disciple. He uses the terms *father*, *children*, and *son*. He describes their relationship with words like *encouraging*, *comforting*, *urging*, and *true son in the faith*.

2. How do Paul's words reinforce what you thought discipleship was?

_____

_____

_____

_____

You are witnesses, and so is God, of how holy, righteous and blameless we were among you who believed. For you know that we dealt with each of you as a father deals with his own children, encouraging, comforting and urging you to live lives worthy of God, who calls you into his kingdom and glory.
(1 Thessalonians 2:10-12)

Paul, an apostle of Christ Jesus by the command of God our Savior and of Christ Jesus our hope,
To Timothy my true son in the faith:
Grace, mercy and peace from God the Father and Christ Jesus our Lord.
(1 Timothy 1:1-2)

Although in Christ I could be bold and order you to do what you ought to do, yet I appeal to you on the basis of love. I then, as Paul—an old man and now also a prisoner of Christ Jesus—I appeal to you for my son Onesimus, who became my son while I was in chains. Formerly he was useless to you, but now he has become useful both to you and to me.
(Philemon 1:8-11)

Characteristics of Spiritual Childhood

Spiritual infants typically see Christianity in terms of "just me and God." Spiritual children, on the other hand, have at least made a basic connection to a spiritual family: a church. They may be young in the faith, or they may have been Christians for years, but all spiritual children have the following characteristics, which are indications of their spiritual immaturity.

- *Self-Centeredness.* We all struggle with selfishness from time to time, but children are self-centered because they are the center of their world and interpret everything from the perspective of "me." Spiritual children are often more concerned about *their* needs than the needs of others. This is why they need a spiritual family to help them begin the process of getting their eyes off themselves.
- *Idealism.* Because they are inexperienced, children tend to be black-and-white in their thinking, as well as naive. For instance, spiritual children might think disciples can listen only to Christian worship music or read nothing but the Bible. When spiritual children apply their idealism to how other Christians should live, it can be disappointing and legalistic. The only one who meets all ideals perfectly is Jesus Christ.
- *Overconfidence or under-confidence.* Spiritual children move back and forth on a confidence continuum. Overconfidence manifests itself as pride. Under-confidence can become self-loathing and defeat. Without intentional guidance from a more mature disciple, spiritual children may swing back and forth on the confidence scale.

3. As you review the characteristics of a spiritual child, do you see any that apply to you? What areas of growth need work in your life?

self - centredness

"The Phrase from the Stage"

Again, we use the term "phrase from the stage" to help disciple-makers learn to listen for clues as to where a disciple may be in his or her development.

4. Check the boxes for the phrases you have heard in your small group or church.

☑ "I believe in Jesus and my church is in the woods, just Him and me."
☐ "Don't branch my group into two groups. It is comfortable for me right now."
☑ "Who are all these new people coming to our church? The church is getting too big."
☑ "I love my small group; don't add any more people to it."
☐ "My small group is not taking care of my needs like they should."
☐ "I don't have anyone who is spending enough time with me. No one is discipling me."
☐ "I didn't like the music today. If they only did it like . . ."

☑ "I am not being fed in my church, so I am going to a church that meets my needs better."

☑ "Pastor looked right at me and didn't even say hello."

A Spiritual Child's Needs

5. Based on what you have read so far in today's lesson, what do you think a spiritual child needs at this stage?

dose of reality & encouragement

6. Compare your ideas with some things that we have found spiritual children need. Check those that are similar to the ones you wrote above.

☐ A relational connection to a church family
☐ Help for how to start feeding themselves spiritually
☐ Teaching about who they are in Christ
☐ Teaching about how to have a relationship with Christ
☐ Teaching about how to have relationships with other believers
☐ Teaching about appropriate expectations concerning other believers

7. What are some ways you could intentionally help the spiritual children around you to grow?

Be prepared to discuss your answers in the small-group session.

Review

- The third stage of spiritual growth is childhood.
- Spiritual children are typically self-centered, idealistic, and prone to struggle with a balance in their confidence.
- Don't fall into the trap of misjudging spiritual maturity by time one spends in church.

day 4

I write to you, dear children, because your sins have been forgiven on account of his name. I write to you, fathers, because you have known him who is from the beginning. I write to you, young men, because you have overcome the evil one.

(1 John 2:12-13)

Stages of growth are all around us. Trees begin as seeds. Ferocious lions begin life as cubs. Human growth and development happens in stages as well. Jesus Himself experienced this physical process of human growth as He went from infancy to adulthood (see Luke 2:52).

God designed spiritual growth to occur in stages as well. He doesn't transform us instantly into mature disciples immediately after conversion and baptism. This week you are going to evaluate your own growth as a disciple. Don't be discouraged if you find some areas needing work. We are all in process. We all have bad days, and we all have weak areas. God uses us despite our flaws, which is both amazing and humbling.

1. After you read 1 John 2:12-13 in the margin, please draw a line matching the characteristic described in the passage with the correct stage of maturity.

Do nothing out of selfish ambition or vain conceit, but in humility consider others better than yourselves. Each of you should look not only to your own interests, but also to the interests of others.

(Philippians 2:3-4)

Be devoted to one another in brotherly love. Honor one another above yourselves. Never be lacking in zeal, but keep your spiritual fervor, serving the Lord. Be joyful in hope, patient in affliction, faithful in prayer. Share with God's people who are in need. Practice hospitality.

(Romans 12:10-13)

This is how we know what love is: Jesus Christ laid down his life for us. And we ought to lay down our lives for our brothers. If anyone has material possessions and sees his brother in need but has no pity on him, how can the love of God be in him? Dear children, let us not love with words or tongue but with actions and in truth.

(1 John 3:16-18)

Stage	Characteristic
Children	Have known Jesus for a long time
Young men	Know that Jesus forgave their sins
Fathers	Have victory over the Devil's temptations

This section of John's letter is not addressing the children's ministry, the youth ministry, and the adult Sunday school, nor is John writing to men only. Instead, he is writing about different stages of spiritual maturity.

Characteristics of a Spiritual Young Adult

The key characteristic for this stage is a God-and-others-centered outlook. This stage covers a wide span of spiritual growth. (Remember, we are talking about *spiritual* characteristics, not *physical* ones. Age is not the criteria.) Spiritual young adults begin to see that God shaped them for a purpose, and as their priorities begin to change, they start looking for a place to serve where they can use their abilities and gifts. They make the sacrifice necessary to serve. As they become more secure in Christ, they are able to overlook the faults of others. They are action-oriented, zealous, and in need of a way to get involved in ministry.

While spiritual infants and children will serve in a church, they will do so as long as the personal benefits outweigh the costs. In contrast, spiritual young adults serve in a church for the glory of God and the good of others.

2. Read the verses in the margin. For each of the following characteristics of the spiritual young adult, write the corresponding Scripture reference:

_____Rom 12_____ Serving others with joy
_____Phil 2_____ Others-centered with humility
_____1 John 3_____ Sacrificing for others

Your answers should be in the following order: Romans 12:10-13; Philippians 2:3-4; 1 John 3:16-18.

"The Phrase from the Stage"

3. Here again, the phrases people use can help us identify spiritual young adulthood. Check the ones you have heard before.

- ☐ "I love my group, but there are others who need a group like this."
- ☐ "I think I could lead a group with a little help. I have three friends I have been witnessing to, and this group would be too big for them."
- ☐ "Look how many are at church today—it's awesome! I had to walk two blocks from the closest parking spot."
- ☐ "Randy and Rachel missed group and I called to see if they are okay. Their kids have the flu, so maybe our group can make meals for them. I'll start."
- ☐ "In my devotions, I came across something I have a question about."
- ☐ "I noticed that we don't have an old folks' visitation team. Do you think I could be involved?"

4. How are these phrases different from the ones a spiritual child or infant would use?

less selfish

Be prepared to discuss your answers in the small-group session.

A Real Life Ministries Story

Jeff began attending one of our small groups. At first he was nervous, hesitant, and self-conscious, but because the members of the group accepted him without reservation, he soon felt that it was a safe place for him. After several weeks, Jeff opened up and talked about his struggles. To his surprise, others began talking about their own struggles, and Jeff discovered that all Christians experience difficulty from time to time. He experienced how disciples encourage and support one another.

Jeff grew as a disciple, and he began to change. When his small group volunteered to pour a cement pad for a widow in the group, Jeff showed up, worked hard, and stayed around to finish the project after several others had to leave. He had also begun meeting with a few people who were struggling with problems.

5. As you think about Jeff's story, review today's Bible verses. How does God bring about a change in perspective from self to others in the life of a maturing disciple?

6. How can we cooperate with that change?

_____

_____

_____

_____

_____

7. Below is a list of what a spiritual young adult needs in order to grow spiritually. Write an "X" by those that you clearly know how to provide or help others with and an "O" by those that you are unclear about. Get clarity from your small group this week.

X or O	Young Adults Need . . .
	A place to learn how to serve
	A spiritual parent who will debrief with them about ministry experiences
	Ongoing relationships that offer encouragement and accountability
	Help for establishing boundaries
	Guidance regarding appropriate expectations of people they will serve
	Help for identifying their gifts
	Skills training

Review

- The fourth stage of spiritual growth is the young adult stage.
- Spiritual young adults are characterized by a change from being focused on self to being focused on God and others.
- Spiritual young adults begin to see that God shaped them for a purpose and their priorities begin to change.

THE SPIRITUAL PARENT

day 5

This is the last stage of a disciple's growth. We purposely use the word *parent* rather than *adult* because a parent is someone who has a child. Spiritual parents reproduce. They intentionally make other disciples who in turn make disciples. While it's true that disciples do not have to wait until they are fully mature before they can make other disciples, intentional disciple-making is characteristic of spiritual parents.

A word of caution: Avoid thinking that any of the stages of discipleship imply levels of greater worth. Parents are not more valuable than infants; all kinds of disciples make up the family of God. They are all precious in His sight. A spiritual parent who mistakenly thinks that he or she has arrived is headed for the pitfall of pride. If anything, growth results in greater responsibility. The stage of spiritual parenthood is where the work really begins.

Characteristics of a Spiritual Parent

A spiritual parent intentionally cooperates with God to reproduce disciples.

1. The following statements are characteristics of disciples. Write "SP" beside the ones that you think apply to spiritual parents:

SP ___ A. They are intentional about building relationships so that discipleship can happen.

___ B. They have a great need to be affirmed and accepted by others.

SP ___ C. They are able to reproduce the process they have learned as a disciple.

SP ___ D. They are able to feed themselves spiritually on God's Word.

___ E. They require lots of close personal attention and protection.

___ F. They are learning to serve, so they need a place to "practice" serving.

SP ___ G. They work within a team of disciples, acknowledging that they do not possess all that a disciple needs to be well-rounded.

This list has a mix of characteristics from different stages of growth. Here they are according to growth stage: spiritual infants—E, spiritual children—B, young adults—F, spiritual parents—A, C, D, and G.

Here are some of the key characteristics of a spiritual parent. They:

- **Reproduce disciples.** Spiritual parents fulfill the command to make disciples. They intentionally build relationships that open doors to lead others to follow Jesus. As disciples grow, spiritual parents prepare to release them to make and train other disciples.
- **Feed themselves.** Spiritual parents understand the Bible well enough that they can get personal nourishment from it. They are ready for meat, yet they know how to give milk to spiritual infants who are just learning about God's Word. Usually if they have a question about the Bible, they know where to find the answer.

2. List three ways disciples can feed themselves from God's Word.

- *memorization*

- *personal study*

- *teaching*

Spiritual parents feed themselves by doing things to keep God's Word in their minds, including these habits: regularly reading and memorizing the Bible, learning Bible stories, listening to sermons, studying the Bible, and regularly discussing Scripture with other disciples.

- **Value the church team.** Spiritual parents are team players committed to seeing the church accomplish its mission. They are keenly aware of their own personal ministry. They work to help the body of Christ be a powerful force for accomplishing the parts of the tasks that require team effort.

"The Phrase from the Stage"

People talk about what they love, and when spiritual parents talk about what God is doing through them, they are not bragging or name-dropping. Their humility is evident.

3. Do you recognize yourself in any of these phrases? Check any that you have said or thought:

- ☐ "This guy at work asked me to go explain the Bible to him. Pray for me."
- ☐ "We get to baptize someone from our small group tonight. When is the next 101 class? I want to get her plugged into ministry somewhere."
- ☐ "Our small group is going on a mission trip, and I have given each person a different responsibility."
- ☐ "I realized discipleship happens at home, too. Will you hold me accountable to spend time discipling my kids?"
- ☐ "I have a person in my small group who is passionate about children. Can you have the children's ministry people call me?"

4. Based on your study this week, circle the part of the diagram that best indicates your level of spiritual growth.

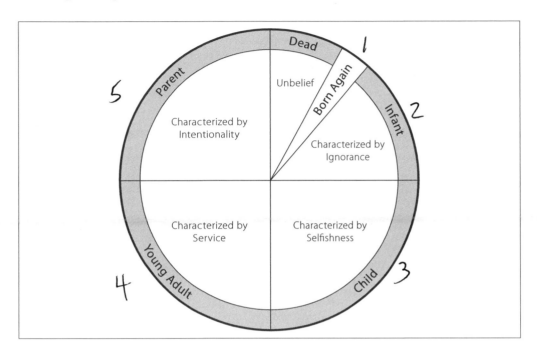

5. How has your assessment of yourself changed since the beginning of the week?

Be prepared to share your answers in your small group this week.

A Spiritual Parent's Needs

Stan had become an effective disciple-maker, but he wanted a break in his routine and decided he would take the summer off. We did not see him again until October. When he returned, he hung his head in shame. His time off had turned into a break from God. He had gotten out of the habit of Bible reading and prayer and had not continued to meet with his accountability partners. Consequently, victories over sin that he had previously experienced had become struggles once again.

6. Based on Stan's story and the passage in the margin, what would you say a spiritual parent needs?

encouragement, accountability

See to it, brothers, that none of you has a sinful, unbelieving heart that turns away from the living God. But encourage one another daily, as long as it is called Today, so that none of you may be hardened by sin's deceitfulness.

(Hebrews 3:12-13)

Lone Rangers often give up or fall into sin because they are isolated. Without the encouragement and accountability of others, our spiritual health is at risk. Even the most mature disciple can get discouraged or fail. A spiritually mature parent knows these truths and works to maintain the following:

- Ongoing relationships with other disciple-makers
- A church family—discipling people as part of a team
- Peer accountability and encouragement

Review

- The final stage of spiritual growth is parenthood.
- Spiritual parents are characterized by the ability to reproduce disciples.
- They are able to feed themselves from God's Word.
- Spiritual parents need encouragement and accountability.

three keys to making disciples

Do you remember the question that began our study? *What does a church look like when it succeeds?* We've spent the past three weeks looking at the biblical basis for how Real Life Ministries answered that question.

1. From week 1, according to Matthew 28:19-20, a church is successful when it obeys the command to _____ _____.

    Matthew 4:19, which gives a clear, uncomplicated picture of what a disciple looks like, can help a church know if it is obeying the command to make disciples.

2. Without looking back at week 2, can you draw a line connecting the three phrases of Matthew 4:19 with the corresponding part of the definition?

"Follow Me"	A disciple is committed to the mission of Christ (hands)
"I will make you"	A disciple knows and follows Christ (head)
"Fishers of men"	A disciple is being changed by Christ (heart)

In week 3, we looked at the stages of growth that every believer moves through on his or her way to becoming a disciple who can disciple others. Beside each stage listed below, write one phrase that a person in that stage might say.

A church is successful when everyone in the church is in the game, maturing into disciples who can reproduce other disciples.

This week we move from the *why* of disciple-making to the *how*. We are going to coach you through the system we have put in place at Real Life Ministries to help our people make disciples. By the end of the week, you will be able to summarize the process.

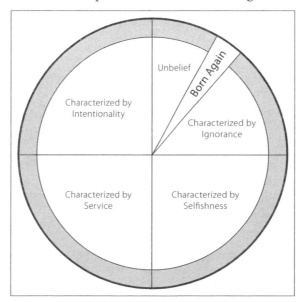

day 1

A SUCCESSFUL JOURNEY

When Bill Krause was eighteen years old, he and some buddies headed from southern Idaho to Seattle. This was before GPS systems were invented, but Bill and his friends came up with what seemed a foolproof navigating strategy: Signs along the road would lead them to Seattle.

They knew they were off course when they noticed they were driving along a set of railroad tracks in the middle of nowhere instead of on the freeway. The nine-hour trip to Seattle turned into twelve. When they finally rolled into the city, things got worse. There were lots of signs, but they did not recognize a single name flying past them as they drove in the dark in the pouring rain. Then things got worse again. The car broke down. Stranded alongside the road, they called a friend to rescue them. When they finally arrived at their destination, it was very late and they were tired and confused. The journey was no fun. Bill and his buddies learned an invaluable road trip lesson: A successful journey requires planning and preparation.

This story illustrates the three key elements that must be present for a successful journey:

A Driver: The Intentional Leader

A road trip cannot begin if someone doesn't turn the key, start the car, and drive. A driver with a destination in mind is essential.

In the discipleship process, we call this driver an **intentional leader**. He or she has to drive the discipleship process toward the goal of making disciples. This driver needs some skills, and it helps if he or she has made the trip before or at least has a dependable map.

A Vehicle: The Relational Environment

A driver, of course, must have something to drive. In discipleship, the vehicle the intentional leader drives is the **relational environment**. Relationships are what God uses to communicate His truth and help people grow. Without relationships, the journey of discipleship is boring and ineffective. It may be informative, but it won't be life-changing. Motivation can die because no one is there to celebrate a breakthrough or support us when we struggle. Relationships create the environment where discipleship happens best.

A Map: The Reproducible Process

The third component for a successful journey is a map. If Bill and his friends had had a map, they would have saved time and energy and been able to track their progress along the way. With a map, Bill could have seen when he was halfway there, and he could have shown the others the best route to take. Using a map virtually eliminates the risk of getting lost.

We call the road map that we use in discipleship the **reproducible process.** This road map allows us to measure a disciple's progress and teach that disciple the route so that he or she can intentionally lead others on the same journey.

1. Write the correct label below each part of a successful journey in the diagram.

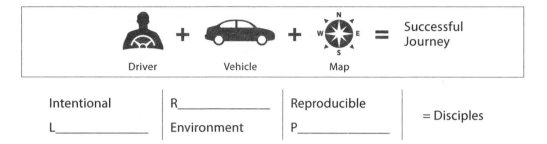

Intentional L_____	R_____ Environment	Reproducible P_____	= Disciples

A Biblical Foundation

The entire discipleship journey has a biblical foundation. In other words, these three elements of the discipleship journey are modeled in Scripture, especially in the life of Jesus and in the early church.

Look at what happened to the disciples after Jesus went back to heaven and sent them the Holy Spirit. We can see the three key elements of the discipleship journey at work in the early church.

2. Read Acts 2:42-46 in the margin. Draw a box around the words showing the intentional leaders. Circle the words indicating a relational environment. Underline the words showing a process that would reproduce disciples.

The apostles were the intentional leaders. The relational environment is inferred because the members of the early church met regularly in homes. The word *fellowship* highlights the importance of these relationships. And the reproducible process for growth? It is not as clear in this passage, but they were having daily meetings and were devoted to the apostles' teaching, breaking bread, and prayer.

These meetings produced growing disciples, as we see later on in the book of Acts, so we know that the apostles were intentionally training up others. We will take a closer look at the reproducible process later this week.

3. How have you experienced each part of this journey to date? Write notes that remind you of the experiences you have already had in your discipleship journey.

- Intentional Leadership

_____
_____
_____
_____

They devoted themselves to the apostles' teaching and to the fellowship, to the breaking of bread and to prayer. Everyone was filled with awe, and many wonders and miraculous signs were done by the apostles. All the believers were together and had everything in common. Selling their possessions and goods, they gave to anyone as he had need. Every day they continued to meet together in the temple courts. They broke bread in their homes and ate together with glad and sincere hearts.
(Acts 2:42-46)

- Relational Environment

  _____
  _____
  _____
  _____

- Reproducible Process

  _____
  _____
  _____
  _____

Be prepared to share your answers with your small group.

Review

The discipleship journey requires three key components:

- An intentional leader
- A relational environment
- A reproducible process

KEY #1: AN INTENTIONAL LEADER   **day 2**

Let's have some fun. Let's say some folks have come to a meeting to find out about leading a discipleship group. You are asked to divide them into two groups: those who have potential to be intentional leaders and those who do not.

1.   Put a check beside any of the following characteristics or circumstances that would not indicate that a person is potentially an intentional leader.

  ☐ Knows the end result that he or she wants and works toward it
  ☐ Hands the leader's guide to someone the day of the group because he or she will be gone
  ☐ Asks for and gives clear instructions when assuming or delegating a task
  ☐ Has a heartfelt desire to give people an opportunity to know Jesus
  ☐ Quickly scans the week's lesson for the first time only minutes before the group meets
  ☐ Looks forward to the day when a disciple will join him or her in the mission of Christ
  ☐ Agrees to lead because no one else will volunteer
  ☐ Refuses to leave to chance another person's growth as a disciple
  ☐ Has an advanced Bible or theology degree

You will compare your list to others during the small-group time.

Leading On Purpose

Early in his ministry, Avery Willis attended a Saturday night Bible study sponsored by The Navigators. After attending for several weeks and questioning the leaders about their methods of discipling people, he convinced the organization's director, Skip Gray, that he was serious about discipleship, so Skip agreed to disciple him.

Every week Skip drove for an hour to spend some time with Avery. He always brought someone with him to disciple on the way, but once there, he met with Avery one on one. Skip had a definite goal in mind for each meeting. He gave Avery assignments and always took time to answer his questions, pray, and hold him accountable to develop the disciplines of a disciple. Skip traveled two hours for an hour of interaction. Though Avery learned only the basics of discipleship before Skip was transferred to another city, here is his lasting impression of Skip's influence in his life: "At the time, I thought I would make that drive to speak to a crowd but doubted I would do it for *one* person. Following Skip's example, I have committed my life to making disciples who make disciples."

2. What did Skip do that shows us who an intentional leader is and what he or she does?

_____

_____

_____

_____

After this the Lord appointed seventy-two others and sent them two by two ahead of him to every town and place where he was about to go.

(Luke 10:1)

When Jesus looked up and saw a great crowd coming toward him, he said to Philip, "Where shall we buy bread for these people to eat?" He asked this only to test him, for he already had in mind what he was going to do.

(John 6:5-6)

Then came the day of Unleavened Bread on which the Passover lamb had to be sacrificed. Jesus sent Peter and John, saying, "Go and make preparations for us to eat the Passover."

"Where do you want us to prepare for it?" they asked.

He replied, "As you enter the city, a man carrying a jar of water will meet you. Follow him to the house that he enters, and say to the owner of the house, 'The Teacher asks: Where is the guest room, where I may eat the Passover with my disciples?' He will show you a large upper room, all furnished. Make preparations there."

They left and found things just as Jesus had told them. So they prepared the Passover.

(Luke 22:7-13)

"Lord, if it's you," Peter replied, "tell me to come to you on the water."

"Come," he said.

Then Peter got down out of the boat, walked on the water and came toward Jesus. But when he saw the wind, he was afraid and, beginning to sink, cried out, "Lord, save me!"

Immediately Jesus reached out his hand and caught him. "You of little faith," he said, "why did you doubt?"

(Matthew 14:28-31)

Here are some possible answers:

- Made sure that Avery wanted to be a disciple
- Developed a personal relationship with Avery
- Had definite goals
- Gave Avery assignments that helped him move forward in his spiritual growth
- Assessed Avery's specific needs as he answered questions
- Held him accountable

Jesus as an Intentional Leader

Jesus spent purposeful time with His disciples and was involved in their daily lives.

3. Read the Scriptures listed in the margin. The following is a list of Jesus' intentional actions. For each action, write the Scripture reference of the verse that describes it.

_____ Jesus sent out a team that had to trust Him by following specific instructions.

_____ Jesus presented a challenge in order to see how His disciples would respond.

_____ Jesus allowed a disciple to fail to teach a lesson about faith.

_____ Jesus organized teams to prepare for the next phase of His ministry.

Your answers should be in the following order: Luke 22:7-13; John 6:5-6; Matthew 14:28-31; Luke 10:1.

Jesus was the master disciple-maker, and we can study His methods and imitate Him. None of us will ever be perfect at making disciples, but we can look to Him as our perfect example.

Intentional leaders move with purpose through their interactions with the people in their small groups and in personal one-on-one meetings to move disciples along the journey. A leader who is intentional in what he or she does drives the work of disciple-making.

4. How intentional was someone to help you in your growth as a disciple of Jesus? Check the answer that is closest to your situation.

☐ I had no one to lead me, so I picked it up on my own.
☐ Those I followed were not as intentional as this lesson teaches.
☐ I had leaders who were very intentional with me.
☐ Even though they were not trained in disciple-making, my leaders were still led by Jesus.
☐ Other _____

Be prepared to discuss your answers with your small group.

At this point, you may be thinking, *I never had anyone intentionally disciple me. How can I disciple anyone else?* If so, don't despair. We wrote this training manual so you would know what to do. Even if you have never been intentionally discipled, you *can* learn to be a disciple-maker.

Review

- A disciple-maker is intentional about accomplishing his or her purpose.
- An intentional leader relates personally to those being discipled.
- An intentional leader follows a plan to bring disciples to maturity.

day 3

KEY #2: A RELATIONAL ENVIRONMENT

Relationships may well be the most sought-after yet most absent piece of the discipleship journey. People are desperate to find relationships, but most are inexperienced at knowing how to nurture them. Please give extra attention to this day.

Without a vehicle, you can't take a road trip. You can have the most skilled driver and the most accurate and user-friendly map as your guide, yet you won't get to your destination if you lack transportation. A relational environment is the vehicle that God uses to bring about real change in people's lives. Without true relationship, discipleship is difficult and rarely successful.

1. What do you think of when you read the term relational environment?

_____

_____

_____

_____

_____

_____

_____

_____

_____

2. How might you evaluate the health of the relational environment in a small group? Select more than one of the following questions you might ask, or write your own.

☐ Are the people friendly?
☐ Are people open and honest with each other?
☐ Do they care beyond the group meeting?
☐ Do they notice when others are gone?
☐ Other questions that reveal relational indicators:

_____

_____

_____

Each of these questions touches on an aspect that contributes to making a relational environment. Today we will summarize a few essentials that you can begin to use right away. In week 6, we will look in depth at this key component of discipleship.

God Is Relational

God's very nature is relational. The doctrine of the Trinity describes a relationship between Father, Son, and Holy Spirit. God's relational nature is communicated throughout the Bible.

3. Read the following passages in your Bible. Write down words that represent the kind of relationship God is depicted as having in each passage.

Scripture	Your Description
Genesis 3:8-9	
Exodus 33:11	
Psalm 36:5-10	
John 15:13	

You might have written words such as *friend, loving, provider,* and *protector.*

Creating a Relational Environment

In order for a group to have a relational environment, the group must be small. Groups aren't small if they have twenty or more people in them. In fact, Jesus had only twelve in His small group, and He invested even more significantly in just three. We believe that small groups of twelve or less are best suited for disciple-making.

4. List a few reasons why you think a smaller group is preferable for making disciples.

_____

_____

_____

_____

_____

The reasons you have listed might have to do with communication, proximity, or even time management. Discuss your answers with your group this week.

The primary reason for keeping a group small is so each person can be known. When our motives are exposed, our lives can be challenged, encouraged, and developed. We cannot be known in a Sunday morning crowd. We cannot really be known by just sharing answers to questions from a training manual about discipleship or talking to someone for five minutes after a Bible study every week.

5. What are the traits or qualities people must possess in order for you to feel safe enough to share your heart with them? List them here.

_____

_____

_____

_____

_____

6. How can intentional leaders cultivate these traits or qualities in a small group?

_____

_____

_____

_____

In order for a small group to have a relational environment, the leader must model transparency and authenticity. These two characteristics set the stage for disciples to draw closer in relationships.

7. Complete the following sentences:

- Someone who is transparent usually tells me . . .

_____

_____

_____

- Someone who is transparent usually listens to me like (or with) . . .

_____

_____

_____

- Someone who is transparent makes me feel . . .

_____

_____

_____

- The behavior that convinces me that someone is an authentic person is . . .

_____

_____

_____

- An authentic person will treat me like (or with) . . .

_____

_____

_____

- When I am around a person who is authentic, I feel . . .

Your answers contain clues to the behaviors and attitudes that intentional leaders need to cultivate in themselves to create a relational environment. You can develop transparency and authenticity if you set your mind to it. It is not for our comfort but rather for the kingdom of God.

Large gatherings provide inspiration and help us pool our resources for the task, but they are not effective for discipleship. Discipleship happens in relationships, such as those that can be formed in a small group. Intentional leaders must remove any roadblocks that might keep them from building meaningful, authentic relationships within their small group.

8. Build the relationships in your current small group. Write a personal affirmation for each person in the group.

  ----

9. What might hinder you from creating a relational environment for those whom you disciple? Write a prayer, asking God to help you remove those roadblocks.

Review

- A small group of twelve people or less is the best environment for disciple-making.
- Discipleship happens best in relationships.
- In a relational environment, the leader models authenticity and transparency.

day 4

Now he had to go through Samaria. So he came to a town in Samaria called Sychar, near the plot of ground Jacob had given to his son Joseph. Jacob's well was there, and Jesus, tired as he was from the journey, sat down by the well. It was about the sixth hour.

When a Samaritan woman came to draw water, Jesus said to her, "Will you give me a drink?" (His disciples had gone into the town to buy food.)

The Samaritan woman said to him, "You are a Jew and I am a Samaritan woman. How can you ask me for a drink?" (For Jews do not associate with Samaritans.)

Jesus answered her, "If you knew the gift of God and who it is that asks you for a drink, you would have asked him and he would have given you living water."

"Sir," the woman said, "you have nothing to draw with and the well is deep. Where can you get this living water? Are you greater than our father Jacob, who gave us the well and drank from it himself, as did also his sons and his flocks and herds?"

Jesus answered, "Everyone who drinks this water will be thirsty again, but whoever drinks the water I give him will never thirst. Indeed, the water I give him will become in him a spring of water welling up to eternal life."

The woman said to him, "Sir, give me this water so that I won't get thirsty and have to keep coming here to draw water."

He told her, "Go, call your husband and come back."

"I have no husband," she replied.

Jesus said to her, "You are right when you say you have no husband. The fact is, you have had five husbands, and the man you now have is not your husband. What you have just said is quite true."

"Sir," the woman said, "I can see that you are a prophet. Our fathers

(continued on page 71)

KEY #3: A REPRODUCIBLE PROCESS

Jesus intended for His disciple-making process to be reproduced. When the twelve accepted Him as Messiah, He invited each of them to join a small group in relationship with Him. As the disciples grew, Jesus gave them responsibilities. In their ministry, He joined them and coached them. Finally He released them to do the same with others.

At Real Life Ministries we have labeled the disciple-making process **share**, **connect**, **minister**, and **disciple** (SCMD). This process is measurable, it is biblically accurate, and it is reproducible.

Share

Intentional disciple-makers interact at the **share** level with people who are spiritually dead or born again and have entered the infant stage of spiritual growth.

With the Spiritually Dead

1. What do you think sharing looks like with those who are spiritually dead? Write your thoughts here.

_____

_____

_____

2. Read John 4:4-26 in the margin, which is the account of Jesus and the woman at the well. Write three things He did to **share** with this woman who was spiritually dead.

_____

_____

_____

Your answers might include the following:

- Jesus asked the woman for a drink.
- He told her of a gift and challenged her to know who He really was.
- He did not condone her lifestyle, yet He affirmed her for being honest with Him.
- As her interest in what He was saying grew, He spoke to her spiritual need and answered her questions.

With Spiritual Infants

When someone we have shared the gospel with believes Jesus for who He is, that person is reborn as a spiritual infant. As disciple-makers, we continue to intentionally **share** with that person new truth, and we also share our lives with him or her. Spiritual infants need our personalized attention, as they will have questions and need to develop new habits. We cannot shove the whole Bible on a spiritual infant's plate. It must be doled out in digestible pieces.

3. Read what Peter says about this stage of discipleship in 1 Peter 2:2-3 in the margin. Write four things that a spiritual baby will need you to share with them.

- ....
- ....
- ....
- ....

You might have written things like answers to spiritual questions, understanding of the Bible, and support to break bad habits. We will look at this more in depth in weeks 7 and 8.

Connect
Spiritual Children

At this stage of spiritual growth, a believer's needs are highly relational. When a disciple arrives at spiritual childhood, he or she needs to connect with a family. To continue to grow, a spiritual child needs connection (which is why at Real Life we encourage everyone to be part of a small group). Spiritual children need to move beyond personalized attention from a spiritual parent and build bonds with Christians from all stages of spiritual growth and maturity.

4. Read Luke 6:12-18 in the margin. Why do you think Jesus singled out twelve followers?

....

....

....

....

....

We believe that Jesus was solidifying the group He was discipling by connecting to them relationally. As the disciple-maker intentionally connects spiritual children to a larger family, the relational environment expands to others. However, the disciple-maker still guides the process.

Minister
Spiritual Young Adults

As they become more aware of God and others, some spiritual young adults are eager to spread their wings and fly. While they are capable of serving in the church, they may lack wisdom in how to go about it. Spiritual young adults still need the steady influence of a spiritual parent, and they need to understand that we make disciples of Jesus, not of ourselves.

Some spiritual children are reluctant to take responsibility and minister to others. When this is the case, a leader must intentionally challenge and encourage the child to grow up. It is essential for spiritual young adults to learn to minister to others or they will not mature. Skipping a stage of growth or bypassing a phase in the process will result in a person who pretends to be spiritually mature, when in fact that person is not.

(continued from page 70)

worshiped on this mountain, but you Jews claim that the place where we must worship is in Jerusalem."

Jesus declared, "Believe me, woman, a time is coming when you will worship the Father neither on this mountain nor in Jerusalem. You Samaritans worship what you do not know; we worship what we do know, for salvation is from the Jews. Yet a time is coming and has now come when the true worshipers will worship the Father in spirit and truth, for they are the kind of worshipers the Father seeks. God is spirit, and his worshipers must worship in spirit and in truth."

The woman said, "I know that Messiah" (called Christ) "is coming. When he comes, he will explain everything to us."

Then Jesus declared, "I who speak to you am he."

(John 4:4-26)

Like newborn babies, crave pure spiritual milk, so that by it you may grow up in your salvation, now that you have tasted that the Lord is good.

(1 Peter 2:2-3)

One of those days Jesus went out to a mountainside to pray, and spent the night praying to God. When morning came, he called his disciples to him and chose twelve of them, whom he also designated apostles: Simon (whom he named Peter), his brother Andrew, James, John, Philip, Bartholomew, Matthew, Thomas, James son of Alphaeus, Simon who was called the Zealot, Judas son of James, and Judas Iscariot, who became a traitor.

He went down with them and stood on a level place. A large crowd of his disciples was there and a great number of people from all over Judea, from Jerusalem, and from the coast of Tyre and Sidon, who had come to hear him and to be healed of their diseases.

(Luke 6:12-18)

Jesus went around teaching from village to village. Calling the Twelve to him, he sent them out two by two and gave them authority over evil spirits.

These were his instructions: "Take nothing for the journey except a staff—no bread, no bag, no money in your belts. Wear sandals but not an extra tunic. Whenever you enter a house, stay there until you leave that town. And if any place will not welcome you or listen to you, shake the dust off your feet when you leave, as a testimony against them."

They went out and preached that people should repent.

(Mark 6:6-12)

Jesus came to them and said, "All authority in heaven and on earth has been given to me. Therefore go and make disciples of all nations, baptizing them in the name of the Father and of the Son and of the Holy Spirit, and teaching them to obey everything I have commanded you. And surely I am with you always, to the very end of the age."

(Matthew 28:18-20)

5. Read Mark 6:7-12 in the margin. In this passage, Jesus is leading His followers into ministry. What strikes you as important?

_____

_____

_____

At this stage, the role of disciple-maker changes from directing to coaching as he or she gives disciples opportunities to serve and then debriefs them in regard to their ministry experiences. One of the goals at this stage is for the disciple to learn personal reliance upon God. Spiritual young adults will make some mistakes while serving, but as we can see from Jesus' example with His disciples, we can turn mistakes into opportunities for learning. Jesus was always close by in case His disciples got in over their heads.

Disciple
Spiritual Parents
In this part of the reproducible process, disciple-makers work with their disciples to help them become independent disciple-makers themselves.

6. Review Matthew 28:18-20 in the margin. Think about it from the vantage point of disciple-makers who are releasing disciples to give others what they have received. What was Jesus' attitude about releasing His disciples?

_____

_____

_____

7. How had Jesus prepared them for this day?

_____

_____

8. What did He say to give confidence to them?

_____

_____

_____

The next few weeks will add to your thoughts on this passage.

Review
- Jesus modeled a reproducible process of discipleship.
- That process included the following:
  - Sharing the gospel with the spiritually dead
  - Sharing your life and basic teaching with spiritual infants
  - Connecting spiritual children in relationships within God's family
  - Helping spiritual young adults to mature through ministry
  - Releasing spiritual parents to disciple others

THE LIMITLESS POTENTIAL OF GOD'S PLAN

day 5

You are now in your fourth week of this study. It is exciting to think about what God will do through you as you make disciples. The tools and insights that are coming up can help you build a legacy of disciple-making that will continue on until Jesus returns.

1. Let's start by matching the growth stage with the appropriate phase of the discipleship process. Using the phases of **share**, **connect**, **minister**, and **disciple**, write the correct phase of the process beside the stage of spiritual growth below:

Spiritually Dead	
Spiritual Infant	
Spiritual Child	
Spiritual Young Adult	
Spiritual Parent	

If you are unsure, go back and check.

God's Plan

God's plan for discipleship unfolds in the book of Acts. Jesus released His disciples to reach the world for Christ. The following words give the outline for the book of Acts:

> You will receive power when the Holy Spirit comes on you; and you
> will be my witnesses in Jerusalem, and in all Judea and Samaria, and
> to the ends of the earth. (Acts 1:8)

The following diagram shows the limitless potential of God's plan as outlined in this verse.

This diagram also illustrates the circles of personal influence that disciples should be reaching: their homes, their workplaces, and their community. In this lesson, we want to focus on the power of discipleship that makes this possible.

The book of Acts is a record of how Acts 1:8 became reality in the first forty years of the church's existence. At the close of Acts, disciples had been made and churches established from Jerusalem, throughout Asia Minor, into Macedonia and Greece,

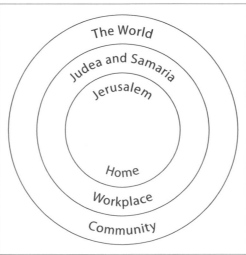

and again across the Adrian Sea clear to Rome. By 300 AD, conservative estimates calculate there were over six million Christians[3] — so many that Emperor Constantine declared Christianity the official religion of the Roman Empire. Jesus' plan worked. These first twelve disciples, empowered and trained by God, transformed the whole world.

Think about it. The message those first disciples gave has even reached you, some two thousand years later and in a very different culture and time than when it was first proclaimed. For twelve men to reach so far, the disciple-making process had to be reproducible.

2. What are some of the reproducible parts of Jesus' disciple-making process?

_____

_____

_____

_____

_____

We will further explore the reproducible process next week, so this question is only intended to get you thinking about the next phase of our study together.

Notice that Jesus did not place an expiration date on His plan to reach the world. His plan is still active today. God is still directing the church to make disciples of every nation.

A few years ago, one of us attended a conference where one of the speakers talked about the state of the church in America. He compared the American church to a flower that sprouted and bloomed during our nation's history but is now dying. He believed that it was time for the church in America to cast its seed to other nations before it completely died. We could not disagree more! The church in America may have forgotten how to make disciples, but that does not mean it must give up. The church comes alive anywhere disciples are being made.

3. Read Romans 8:29-32, Matthew 16:16-18, and 2 Corinthians 4:7-9 in the margin and answer these questions:

- What can stop the mission of Christ?

  _____

  _____

  _____

- Who can stop the mission of Christ?

  _____

  _____

  _____

  _____

Those God foreknew he also predestined to be conformed to the likeness of his Son, that he might be the firstborn among many brothers. And those he predestined, he also called; those he called, he also justified; those he justified, he also glorified.

What, then, shall we say in response to this? If God is for us, who can be against us? He who did not spare his own Son, but gave him up for us all—how will he not also, along with him, graciously give us all things?

(Romans 8:29-32)

Simon Peter answered, "You are the Christ, the Son of the living God."

Jesus replied, "Blessed are you, Simon son of Jonah, for this was not revealed to you by man, but by my Father in heaven. And I tell you that you are Peter, and on this rock I will build my church, and the gates of Hades will not overcome it."

(Matthew 16:16-18)

We have this treasure in jars of clay to show that this all-surpassing power is from God and not from us. We are hard pressed on every side, but not crushed; perplexed, but not in despair; persecuted, but not abandoned; struck down, but not destroyed.

(2 Corinthians 4:7-9)

The power of the mission of Christ is evident from Scripture as well as world history. Imbedded in the disciple-making process is great potential. If a disciple makes a disciple who can make disciples, mathematically the process might look something like this:

- One disciple makes three disciple-makers every five years.
- If those disciples do the same every five years, in ten years there will be almost 180,000 disciple-makers.
- If they continue, in seventy years (less than the average life span) there are potentially fourteen billion disciple-makers. That is twice the number of people currently occupying our planet.

Certainly not everyone will choose to follow Jesus, and some disciple-makers will go to heaven before the seventy years are up, but the point is this: Disciple-making is based upon multiplication, not addition. God's plan for disciple-making has limitless potential. So the real question is, what is holding us back?

4. What holds you back from making three disciple-makers in the next five years? Write your thoughts here.

_____

_____

_____

_____

5. What three actions can you take this year to begin making disciples intentionally?

_____

_____

_____

_____

Be prepared to discuss your answers with your group this week.

Review
- Acts 1:8 gives a description of the power and potential of disciple-making.
- History and Scripture indicate that nothing can stop Christ's mission to make disciples.
- The math of disciple-making is exponential.

how to be an intentional leader

Some people are intimidated by the title *leader*; others are eager to take charge. How does it strike you? We use the label *intentional leader* interchangeably with *disciple-maker*. We don't see Jesus leading by accident, nor do we believe He was haphazard in His approach. As a disciple-maker, He intentionally led His followers.

INTENTIONAL LEADERS IMITATE JESUS

day 1

Many willing Christians have absolutely no plan for disciple-making. Some even spiritualize their lack of intention as if it leaves more room for God to be at work. Others follow a curriculum but have no idea *how* to make disciples. Jesus had a plan but was not limited by a curriculum.

Let's look closer at His intentional leadership.

1. Read the story of Jesus feeding five thousand people (see John 6:2-14 in the margin). Underline the question that Jesus asked in verse 5. The next verse describes Jesus being intentional as He trained His disciples.

2. Write John 6:6 below:

_____

_____

_____

_____

3. Jesus knew what He intended to teach before He asked Philip the question. Name one lesson that the people, the boy, or the disciples learned from Jesus that day.

_____

_____

_____

_____

You might have written down one of the following: the people learned that Jesus was a prophet; the boy learned that Jesus could transform a little into a lot; Jesus' disciples saw proof that He was the Son of God. They also grew in their understanding of what it meant to be His disciple.

A great crowd of people followed him because they saw the miraculous signs he had performed on the sick. Then Jesus went up on a mountainside and sat down with his disciples. The Jewish Passover Feast was near.

When Jesus looked up and saw a great crowd coming toward him, he said to Philip, "Where shall we buy bread for these people to eat?" He asked this only to test him, for he already had in mind what he was going to do.

Philip answered him, "Eight months' wages would not buy enough bread for each one to have a bite!"

Another of his disciples, Andrew, Simon Peter's brother, spoke up, "Here is a boy with five small barley loaves and two small fish, but how far will they go among so many?"

Jesus said, "Have the people sit down." There was plenty of grass in that place, and the men sat down, about five thousand of them. Jesus then took the loaves, gave thanks, and distributed to those who were seated as much as they wanted. He did the same with the fish.

(continued on page 78)

(continued from page 77)

When they had all had enough to eat, he said to his disciples, "Gather the pieces that are left over. Let nothing be wasted." So they gathered them and filled twelve baskets with the pieces of the five barley loaves left over by those who had eaten.

After the people saw the miraculous sign that Jesus did, they began to say, "Surely this is the Prophet who is to come into the world."

(John 6:2-14)

Jesus entered Jericho and was passing through. A man was there by the name of Zacchaeus; he was a chief tax collector and was wealthy. He wanted to see who Jesus was, but being a short man he could not, because of the crowd. So he ran ahead and climbed a sycamore-fig tree to see him, since Jesus was coming that way.

When Jesus reached the spot, he looked up and said to him, "Zacchaeus, come down immediately. I must stay at your house today." So he came down at once and welcomed him gladly.

All the people saw this and began to mutter, "He has gone to be the guest of a 'sinner.'"

But Zacchaeus stood up and said to the Lord, "Look, Lord! Here and now I give half of my possessions to the poor, and if I have cheated anybody out of anything, I will pay back four times the amount."

Jesus said to him, "Today salvation has come to this house, because this man, too, is a son of Abraham. For the Son of Man came to seek and to save what was lost."

(Luke 19:1-10)

4. Read the story of Zacchaeus in Luke 19:1-10 in the margin. What are two things Jesus did intentionally to make a disciple out of Zacchaeus?

- *singled out*
  invited himself

-

Jesus *intentionally* singled out Zacchaeus from the crowd. He also invited Himself to Zacchaeus's home. When others grumbled about the tax collector, Jesus purposefully announced that salvation had come to Zacchaeus's home and that He came to seek and save lost people.

5. There is yet another layer of intentional disciple-making in this story: What was Jesus teaching the disciples who were already following Him?

Among other things, the disciples clearly heard Jesus express His mission, and they were witnesses to how He dealt with grumblers who criticized Him. The classroom was Zacchaeus's house, and the lesson included Jesus' love for lost people.

These lessons were not accidents. Jesus did not begin the day saying, "Well, boys, I wonder what we will learn today." He did not seat them in a circle and throw out the comment "Does anybody have anything to share?" Jesus knew what His disciples needed to learn. He intentionally cooperated with His Father, which was an important lesson for the disciples to learn.

6. What was Zacchaeus doing that caused Jesus to single him out of the crowd?

seeking to see him

7. How did Zacchaeus's climbing to the top of a tree help Jesus see that His Father already was at work in the tax collector's life?

In this situation, the disciples saw Jesus identify where His Father was already at work. Zacchaeus climbed the tree because he was eager to see Jesus; God was already drawing him to the kingdom. That day, the disciples watched Jesus join His Father's work to reach an already-searching Zacchaeus.

Intentional but Not Rigid

Being an intentional leader does not mean controlling every possible distraction so that we can execute the perfect lesson plan. Jesus was flexible. He met people on their level without sacrificing His intention to make disciples. People grow at different rates. An intentional leader adjusts his or her approach but continues to deliberately make disciples.

8. Read the passages in the margin and circle what stage of spiritual growth you think Jesus was addressing. Refer to week 3 for the stages of spiritual growth.

John 12:1-3,7-8   Mary Anoints Jesus' Feet

Spiritually Dead	Infant	Child	Young Adult	Parent

Mark 9:20-24   Healing Possessed Boy

Spiritually Dead	Infant	Child	Young Adult	Parent

John 21:15-17   Peter and Jesus by the Sea

Spiritually Dead	Infant	Child	Young Adult	Parent

Jesus adjusted His plan in order to meet people where they were. By anointing Jesus' feet, Mary revealed her heart, showing that she was not self-centered but rather Christ-centered and willing to serve Him. Her behavior was that of a spiritual young adult. The Bible does not specifically state, "And Jesus spoke to the spiritual young adult," but He purposefully defends Mary's actions and encourages her faith.

The father who cried, "Help my unbelief," was desperate and confused about Christ. His behavior was similar to how a spiritual infant or child would react. Jesus adjusted His approach to help the man grow as a disciple. Jesus did not declare, "Since you are a spiritual infant, I will heal your son." He led the discussion to meet the man where he was.

When Peter and Jesus talked by the sea, Jesus spoke to him as a spiritual young adult who was becoming a parent. Jesus challenged Peter to care for His followers (sheep). He directed him to join Him in ministry and even hinted at Peter continuing without Jesus.

In all three cases, Jesus adjusted His leadership to the person's needs. Being intentional does not mean using a rigid, preprogrammed approach, nor does it mean being accidental. Intentional leaders drive the discipleship process. They do not leave it to chance or random luck.

Review
- The discipleship journey requires an intentional leader.
- Jesus modeled being intentional.
- Jesus adapted His plan to the needs of the person.

Six days before the Passover, Jesus arrived at Bethany, where Lazarus lived, whom Jesus had raised from the dead. Here a dinner was given in Jesus' honor. Martha served, while Lazarus was among those reclining at the table with him. Then Mary took about a pint of pure nard, an expensive perfume; she poured it on Jesus' feet and wiped his feet with her hair. And the house was filled with the fragrance of the perfume. . . .

"Leave her alone," Jesus replied. "It was intended that she should save this perfume for the day of my burial. You will always have the poor among you, but you will not always have me."

(John 12:1-3,7-8)

They brought him. When the spirit saw Jesus, it immediately threw the boy into a convulsion. He fell to the ground and rolled around, foaming at the mouth.

Jesus asked the boy's father, "How long has he been like this?"

"From childhood," he answered. "It has often thrown him into fire or water to kill him. But if you can do anything, take pity on us and help us."

"'If you can'?" said Jesus. "Everything is possible for him who believes."

Immediately the boy's father exclaimed, "I do believe; help me overcome my unbelief!"

(Mark 9:20-24)

When they had finished eating, Jesus said to Simon Peter, "Simon son of John, do you truly love me more than these?"

"Yes, Lord," he said, "you know that I love you."

Jesus said, "Feed my lambs."

Again Jesus said, "Simon son of John, do you truly love me?"

He answered, "Yes, Lord, you know that I love you."

Jesus said, "Take care of my sheep."

The third time he said to him, "Simon son of John, do you love me?"

Peter was hurt because Jesus asked him the third time, "Do you love me?" He said, "Lord, you know all things; you know that I love you."

Jesus said, "Feed my sheep."

(John 21:15-17)

day 2

INTENTIONAL LEADERS UNDERSTAND THE GAME

Have you ever watched young kids play Little League baseball? An outfielder picks dandelions, while the third baseman is distracted by a jet in the sky. Occasionally, a child gets a hit, and the crowd cheers. When a child catches a fly ball, they roar. Yet these kids won't master the game on their own. They can stand on the field, wear uniforms, and even catch a ball, but that does not ensure they are learning the game of baseball. They need someone who knows the game—a coach—to teach them.

1. Who taught you your favorite sport or hobby? *self taught :)*

_____

_____

2. How well did he or she know "the game"?

_____

_____

A good baseball coach will know more than just how to catch a fly ball. Effective coaches know more than just a piece of the game. The same is true of disciple-makers. We can't just add water to some prepackaged discipleship mix and stir until a disciple is made. Whether you are a parent, small-group leader, Sunday school teacher, or pastor, God is bringing people into your path whom you can disciple. But to be an intentional leader/coach, you must know the game.

In discipleship, understanding "the game" means understanding the spiritual battle, maintaining a biblical worldview, and avoiding an overdependence on classroom settings. Here is a brief overview of what disciple-makers need to know about "the game."

Understanding the Spiritual Battle

Disciple-makers need to understand the spiritual realities behind the world we live in. Christians are in a spiritual battle for souls against an enemy that seeks to destroy everyone.

Roman soldiers in full armor were a common sight in Paul's day. Paul used the image of armor to help us understand this spiritual battle.

3. Pick two items from Paul's description in Ephesians 6:13-17 (in the margin) and explain how a disciple-maker might use these items intentionally to make disciples. (Example: The truth-belt holds armor and weapons in place; therefore, disciple-makers use the truth to keep their message pure and its defense secure.)

Put on the full armor of God, so that when the day of evil comes, you may be able to stand your ground, and after you have done everything, to stand. Stand firm then, with the belt of truth buckled around your waist, with the breastplate of righteousness in place, and with your feet fitted with the readiness that comes from the gospel of peace. In addition to all this, take up the shield of faith, with which you can extinguish all the flaming arrows of the evil one. Take the helmet of salvation and the sword of the Spirit, which is the word of God.
(Ephesians 6:13-17)

Item	The Disciple-Maker's Use
1. *Belt of truth*	
2. *Sword – Bible*	

Be ready to discuss your answers this week in your small group.

The battle between heaven and hell is real. All paths do not lead to God. The eternal destinies of fathers, mothers, children, friends, and coworkers are at stake. It is foolish to hope that a new Christian will figure this out without coaching.

Maintaining a Biblical Worldview

Understanding the mind of God and mastering His Word are lifelong endeavors. Our playbook is the Bible, but we don't have to know *everything* about the Bible before we can make disciples. Intentional leaders *work* to build and maintain a biblical worldview in order to better understand the game and make disciples.

4. The following are worldview basics. Using the Bible, which of these questions could you answer?

☐ Where did we come from?
☐ Why is our world so troubled and violent?
☑ Isn't there more than one way to God?
☐ Is there such a thing as a moral absolute? Doesn't culture dictate right and wrong?
☐ Is the Bible an accurate and reliable source of God's truth?
☐ What happens after this life?
☐ Is hell real?
☐ What is the purpose of our lives?

Take time in this week's small group to discuss answers to these questions.

If you want to win at making disciples, you must understand the game—so build your worldview around God's Word. Knowing the Bible is like knowing the rules as well as the playbook. Each "player" needs help to learn how to use these tools in discipleship.

Avoiding Dependence on a Formal Classroom

Understanding the game also means avoiding dependence on a classroom. An effective disciple-maker knows how to take discipleship from theory to practice, from the classroom to the living room. When disciple-making is reduced to a program, people often fail to connect it to a lifestyle. People can be conditioned to follow a list or lesson plan, therefore missing the relationships and dynamics of what it means to grow disciples.

We often witness this confusion when teaching classes to church leaders. During sessions about the process Jesus used for making disciples, we continually field questions about the day-to-day "how tos" of disciple-making. When we challenge the class to give details on discipleship, few of the leaders do more than speculate. Few, if any, offer specific, tangible ways of making disciples because most have never done it. They have only attended a class or followed a curriculum. They knew the theory of the game but had no plan to intentionally make disciples. Most confess that they have never been discipled.

5. Jesus spoke to this in Luke 6:39-40. Please read the passage in the margin. According to Jesus, whom will the student be like?

The _____teacher_____

Can a blind man lead a blind man? Will they not both fall into a pit? A student is not above his teacher, but everyone who is fully trained will be like his teacher.
(Luke 6:39-40)

You should have written the word *teacher*. Discipleship is not a curriculum or a program; it is a lifestyle.

6. Has it hit you yet? How seriously do you take this spiritual battle?

_____

_____

_____

_____

7. How important is it that you know "the game"?

_____

_____

_____

_____

8. Why is it important that discipleship become a lifestyle?

_____

_____

_____

_____

Be prepared to share your answers with your small group.

Review

- Jesus' example calls us to be intentional leaders who understand the game.
- Understanding the game means understanding the spiritual battle, maintaining a biblical worldview, and avoiding overdependence on classes or curriculum.

INTENTIONAL LEADERS EVALUATE THE PLAYERS

day 3

Rookies as well as veteran players need help to reach their full potential. Winning coaches evaluate a player's weaknesses in order to strengthen them. They also assess a player's talents in order to place the player where he or she will benefit the team most. These principles from sports apply in discipleship as well. Effective disciple-makers intentionally evaluate the players.

1. List some things you think an intentional leader should look for when evaluating disciples.

Consistency, ability to listen

Come back and compare your list with what you learn in this lesson.

What to Look For

When a coach evaluates a player's current ability, it helps the coach know what areas the player needs to work on. Likewise, the first thing a disciple-maker does to evaluate a player is identify what growth stage a disciple is in. Expecting a spiritual infant to teach a Bible class is like requiring a toddler to pitch in baseball. Giving people opportunities that align with their maturity prepares them better to grow to the next stage.

2. For each statement, check the box that identifies the disciple's stage of growth. If you need to, refer to the appendix for a summary of each stage.

Disciple 1 – "When you asked us to find Matthew 4:19 in our Bibles, I did not know where to start."

☐ Spiritually Dead   ☐ Infant   ☐ Child   ☐ Young Adult   ☐ Parent

Disciple 2 – "Louise is having surgery this week. I would like to organize meals for the family."

☐ Spiritually Dead   ☐ Infant   ☐ Child   ☐ Young Adult   ☐ Parent

Disciple 3 – "This small group really accepts me. I hope it never changes."

☐ Spiritually Dead   ☐ Infant   ☐ Child   ☐ Young Adult   ☐ Parent

A coach also evaluates the players by studying their abilities to determine their best fit on the team. The answers above are: 1 – Infant, 2 – Young Adult, 3 – Child. Disciple-makers must evaluate the disciple's aptitudes — their gifts, talents, and abilities — in order to help place them where they can best serve God's team. The disciple-maker watches to see what disciples are naturally drawn to in order to identify strengths they might have.

The discipling leader intentionally pictures ways that a disciple's talents could contribute to the mission.

Jesus with His Disciples

Disciple-makers are more likely to accurately evaluate their disciples' growth stages and aptitudes if they spend time together. If Jesus had interacted with His disciples only once a week, for one hour, His impact on them would have diminished greatly. Jesus modeled relationship by being with His disciples. To be intentional and relational as a leader, you must spend time around those you are discipling.

Some people believe that evaluation is done best through questionnaires or aptitude tests, but none of these can replace face-to-face interaction. The only way intentional leaders can get to know their players is to be in relationship with them. This requires time together.

3. What would it require of you to spend time with those you are discipling?

_____

_____

_____

_____

They came to Capernaum. When he was in the house, he asked them, "What were you arguing about on the road?" But they kept quiet because on the way they had argued about who was the greatest.

Sitting down, Jesus called the Twelve and said, "If anyone wants to be first, he must be the very last, and the servant of all."

He took a little child and had him stand among them. Taking him in his arms, he said to them, "Whoever welcomes one of these little children in my name welcomes me; and whoever welcomes me does not welcome me but the one who sent me."

(Mark 9:33-37)

4. Read Mark 9:33-37 in the margin. How did being together with the disciples set up Jesus' teaching?

_____

_____

_____

The answer is that by spending time with the disciples, Jesus was able to respond to where they were in their growth as His followers. As they traveled the road, He observed their behavior, listened to their discussions, and understood their motives. Jesus called out their argument and gave them a lesson that fit the situation perfectly. It pointed them to greater truth about discipleship: "If anyone wants to be first, he must be the very last, and the servant of all" (Mark 9:35).

A disciple's life should not be characterized by struggles over position or control.

Listening to Disciples

While He was with them, Jesus listened to what the disciples were saying so that He could teach them what they needed to learn. Disciple-makers must do the same. As people grow, their comments reveal a great deal about what stage of spiritual growth they are in. At Real Life Ministries we refer to these kinds of statements as "the phrase from the stage."

As you listen to someone you are discipling, ask yourself if the person is:

- Confused about truth (infant)?
- Using self-centered language (child)?
- Making statements that tell me he or she cares about others and is maturing in the faith (young adult)?

Helping People Find Their Fit

Paying attention to what people do and say will help you guide them to find their fit on the team. An intentional leader watches and listens so that he can help people find a place to play in ministry that fits their gifts and abilities.

5. The following list contains needs that present themselves in a small group. These needs offer opportunities for disciples to grow by serving the group and its members. Beside each need, write one or two abilities or aptitudes that an intentional leader might look for in a disciple in order to fit them to that need.

Need	Characteristics or Aptitudes
Someone to facilitate group discussions when the leader is not able to be there.	*Leadership*
Someone to do minor home repair for elderly people in the group.	
Someone to visit people who are in the hospital.	*mercy*
Someone to lead a prayer night for the group.	

Helping people find a fit on the team is not too hard if you are intentional about evaluating your players' aptitudes and gifts. A group facilitator would need to be a good listener. Someone with construction experience could help with minor home repairs. Those who possess compassion are great at hospital calls. Leading a prayer night requires organization as well as prayer. All of these needs become opportunities to make disciples.

We want to be clear that when a disciple-maker evaluates a disciple's stage of spiritual growth, it is not for the purpose of ranking that person's value. Doing so would be harmful. Each disciple comes with a unique set of skills and gifts. Good coaches intentionally evaluate their players so they can help them grow. As they evaluate and train the players, their team begins to win.

6. What do you need to do to be more intentional about evaluating the players?

_____

_____

_____

_____

Review
- Intentional leaders evaluate their players' level of maturity and skill.
- Accurate evaluation requires spending time with people.
- All of this happens in the context of a relationship with your "players."

day 4

INTENTIONAL LEADERS CREATE AN ENVIRONMENT FOR GROWTH

Bill Krause's Sunday school class was well attended, but when he accepted a job at another church and moved away, the class dwindled. People had learned a lot about the Bible, but the class died when Bill left.

Why? Bill admits that he did not hand off duties and responsibilities. He did it all, even setting up the room. He was the star player. No one else ever got in the game. He had trained them to be only spectators.

Effective disciple-makers know they shouldn't do everything, as that will stunt their disciples' growth. They know what needs to happen for an individual disciple to grow and serve, so they create an environment that will help the disciple develop and improve.

1. How might things have turned out differently if Bill had looked for capable people and involved them in the planning and teaching of the class and used those opportunities to make disciples? Circle True (T) or False (F)

> T (F) The class would stop learning the Bible.
> (T) F The class would have had a qualified leader in place before he left.
> T (F) The class would have lost members immediately because Bill wasn't the only one leading.
> (T) F New leaders would have grown up.

The correct answers above are F, T, F, and T.

It was he who gave some to be apostles, some to be prophets, some to be evangelists, and some to be pastors and teachers, to prepare God's people for works of service, so that the body of Christ may be built up until we all reach unity in the faith and in the knowledge of the Son of God and become mature, attaining to the whole measure of the fullness of Christ.

Then we will no longer be infants, tossed back and forth by the waves, and blown here and there by every wind of teaching and by the cunning and craftiness of men in their deceitful scheming.
(Ephesians 4:11-14)

2. Read Ephesians 4:11-14 in the margin. Use it to fill in the blanks.

God gave intentional leaders to the church to ___equip___ God's people for works of ___service___.

Paul provides clarity for disciple-makers. He taught leaders to strengthen people so that they could fulfill their roles in the body of Christ. We would say it this way: "Coach people so that they learn to be effective players who accomplish their role. Prepare them for the purpose of obeying Christ's command to make disciples" (see Matthew 28:18-20).

A Place to Play

Intentional leaders give disciples the opportunity and responsibility of service. That's what Jesus did: He gave His disciples *a place to play.*

3. Read the following passages (in the margin) and answer the accompanying questions.

- What role did the disciples play in feeding the people? (see John 6:5-11)

_____

_____

_____

- What did Jesus send the seventy-two disciples out to do? (see Luke 10:8-12)

_____

_____

_____

- What responsibility did Jesus give to Peter and John for the Passover? (see Luke 22:7-13)

_____

_____

_____

_____

In each case, Jesus met the needs of those around Him, but He also intentionally created opportunities for His disciples to serve. Serving produces players, not spectators. Service helps a disciple develop and mature.

Coaches Create Environments to Win

As a wrestling coach Jim taught the three areas of skill a wrestler needs in order to win:

- Top—starting above your opponent
- Bottom—starting beneath your opponent
- Neutral—both wrestlers on their feet

Most wrestlers have skill in one area, some in two, but few in all three. To win consistently, all three skill sets are needed. A good coach will evaluate the wrestlers' weaknesses and then organize practices so that boys are working on the skills they need to improve.

4. Disciple-makers need to do something similar. Go back to the definition of a disciple (see Matthew 4:19). What three areas of a disciple are addressed in the definition?

_____head_____ - level (primarily information and Bible knowledge)

_____ - level (character and relational skills)

_____hands____ - level (ministry skills and abilities)

All three are needed to make disciples, but each one is developed differently.

When Jesus looked up and saw a great crowd coming toward him, he said to Philip, "Where shall we buy bread for these people to eat?" He asked this only to test him, for he already had in mind what he was going to do.

Philip answered him, "Eight months' wages would not buy enough bread for each one to have a bite!"

Another of his disciples, Andrew, Simon Peter's brother, spoke up, "Here is a boy with five small barley loaves and two small fish, but how far will they go among so many?"

Jesus said, "Have the people sit down." There was plenty of grass in that place, and the men sat down, about five thousand of them. Jesus then took the loaves, gave thanks, and distributed to those who were seated as much as they wanted. He did the same with the fish.

(John 6:5-11)

When you enter a town and are welcomed, eat what is set before you. Heal the sick who are there and tell them, "The kingdom of God is near you." But when you enter a town and are not welcomed, go into its streets and say, "Even the dust of your town that sticks to our feet we wipe off against you. Yet be sure of this: The kingdom of God is near." I tell you, it will be more bearable on that day for Sodom than for that town.

(Luke 10:8-12)

Then came the day of Unleavened Bread on which the Passover lamb had to be sacrificed. Jesus sent Peter and John, saying, "Go and make preparations for us to eat the Passover."

"Where do you want us to prepare for it?" they asked.

He replied, "As you enter the city, a man carrying a jar of water will meet you. Follow him to the house that he enters, and say to the owner of the house, 'The Teacher asks: Where is the guest room, where I may eat the Passover with my disciples?' He will show you a large upper room, all furnished. Make preparations there."

They left and found things just as Jesus had told them. So they prepared the Passover.

(Luke 22:7-13)

5. Place an "X" on the line where you think your strengths are. Ask someone close to you to score your strengths. Discuss the differences.

Head-level *Follow*

1	2	3	4	5	6	7	8	9	10

Heart-level *Be Changed*

1	2	3	4	5	6	7	8	9	10

Hands-level *On Mission*

1	2	3	4	5	6	7	8	9	10

6. If you are all head and no heart, that is a problem. Balance and growth in all areas helps you mature as a disciple. What are some possible coaching tips that might help you improve your weakness?

_____

_____

_____

_____

7. What will you do to work on one area?

_____

_____

_____

_____

The relational environment Jesus created (and we strive to recreate) helps us ensure that discipleship happens. A relational environment offers the best place to challenge a disciple and also provides a place for the disciple to practice.

If you had no intentional leader to coach you, the idea of a safe relational environment in which to grow is probably high on your list. Be a coach who gets disciples in the game.

Review
- Disciples need a coach as they "play the game."
- Giving disciples an active role helps them learn and mature.

UNDERSTANDING GOD'S ROLE, OUR ROLE, AND THE DISCIPLE'S ROLE

day 5

A men's group in our church made a commitment to go deeper as disciples. The next time the group met, the leader shared his past and revealed areas of his life where he had struggled. Others opened up as well, but some men still talked about only football and work. When challenged to go deeper, they made excuses and found reasons to miss meetings. Even when God allowed circumstances in their lives to reveal how broken their families were, these men continued to avoid opening up to the group.

The leader was frustrated and felt he had failed, but that was not the case. He had played his role well. God was definitely at work, revealing to the men their need for Him, but some refused to accept the invitation. They chose shallow acquaintance over real relationship, and the group disbanded.

The material we are studying today convinced that leader not to quit. Eventually he restarted the group, and it has become a healthy discipleship group that continues to meet. It has given birth to two other groups as well.

This disciple-maker understood that he *had* fulfilled his role. He realized that even the best intentional leader cannot make people be relational against their will. We can only do our best to create an environment where relationships can happen.

Only Responsible for Our Role

The story of Philip and the Ethiopian eunuch (see Acts 8:26-40) helps us see that when it comes to disciple-making, whether someone grows as a disciple is not up to only the leader; God plays a role in all spiritual growth, as does the disciple.

1. Read in your Bible Acts 8:26-40, noting the parts that God, Philip, and the Ethiopian eunuch play. Then read the statements below. Put "G" for God's role, "P" for Philip's, and "E" for the Ethiopian's.

_____ The Holy Spirit told Philip to go to the carriage.
_____ Philip ran to the carriage.
_____ Philip asked the Ethiopian questions.
_____ The Ethiopian invited Philip to join him in the carriage.
_____ Philip shared about who Jesus was.
_____ The Ethiopian was convicted to be baptized.
_____ Philip baptized the Ethiopian.

Your answers should look like the following: G, P, P, E, P, G, P.

Having a clear picture of our role is like having a job description. It helps us stay focused on our responsibilities and tells us what we should count on from others.

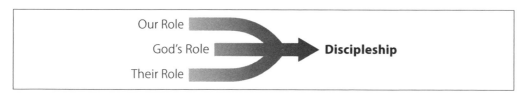

89

A Case Study

Nine guys gather into a small living room at 5:30 a.m. They have just listened to the story of the prodigal son (see Luke 15) and are discussing this story. Ben, the leader, asks, "Who are you in this story?"

Cliff shares that he feels like one of the servants who informed the older brother that the celebration was not for him. Dave, a new Christian, says he still feels like one of the party friends back in town. Everybody chuckles, but they get the point.

Tom is unusually quiet. He leans back in his chair and tries to disengage from the group. The story has cut deep into his heart, and he doesn't want to speak because he knows he will cry. The letter he had just received from his son is still stinging. *Wow*, he thinks to himself, *I wasn't at all like the father waiting for his son. I was so clueless that I ignored his rebellion and tried to pretend everything was all right*. In the letter, Tom's son had told him how he wasn't there when he needed him and how angry he was at him.

Ben notices Tom's body language and directs the question his way but is met with the response of "I don't know." He probes deeper: "Tom, is that all, or is there more? Are you all right?" At that, Tom breaks. He tells the whole story to the group and confesses that today's discussion was too close to home. They pause and pray.

The next few minutes are spent with several guys offering encouragement and suggestions for what Tom could do to rebuild his relationship with his son. The group ends with handshakes and hugs. Ben knows that God is at work using this Bible story to change a disciple.

2. Let's evaluate what happened in this scenario.

What was God doing?

_____

_____

_____

What was the leader's role?

_____

_____

_____

What was the disciple's role?

_____

_____

_____

Here are some key points you may have covered in your answers:

God's Part
- Prompts Tom to go to the meeting that morning
- Uses Luke 15 to speak to Tom
- Uses group to encourage Tom

The Leader's Part
- Tells the prodigal story
- Notices Tom's tension
- Gently probes Tom

The Disciple's Part
- Attends at 5:30 a.m.
- Listens to the story
- Shares his story

Intentional leaders are responsible for only their role in the disciple-making process. If they try to perform God's role or the disciple's role, they will be frustrated. When we know what we are responsible for, it helps us remain intentional and focused.

Review
- A disciple-maker needs to know three roles that are at play in the group: God's role, the leader's role, and the disciple's role.

a closer look at a relational environment

Everyone was surprised when Dan announced he was leaving his wife of twenty years for another woman. He had been meeting with the same group of men for five years. In all that time, Dan never mentioned that he and his wife were having problems. One fellow commented, "I thought we were brothers, but it turns out that we didn't even know each other." They had discussed politics and sports repeatedly, but they did not have real relationships, nor had they grown as disciples. No one led the group any deeper than small talk. It's a true story, and a tragic one at that. How could this happen?

Real relationships are an essential part of God's plan. The world's need for relationships is God's opportunity to build disciples. But these personal relationships cannot happen from a distance or in a crowd. Disciples are made in relationship with other disciples. Remember, a relational environment is the vehicle best suited for discipleship. It allows strangers and acquaintances to become a discipleship family.

SMALL-GROUP PRIORITY

day 1

Spiritual growth happens best with others who share the goal of being a disciple of Jesus.

Read 2 Timothy 2:1-2 in the margin. Paul wrote this to Timothy, a man he discipled. Underline the following words in the passage: *many witnesses*, *reliable men*, and *others*. What do all these words have in common? They are talking about a group of people—about more than one person. The most compelling phrase is *entrust to reliable men*.

Paul's direction to Timothy infers that he would be discipling people, just as Jesus had done and just as Paul had done with Timothy and others (see Acts 16:3,6,13; 17:14-15). Paul was with his disciples in a variety of situations and places, not just in a classroom where Paul lectured.

Be strong in the grace that is in Christ Jesus. And the things you have heard me say in the presence of many witnesses entrust to reliable men who will also be qualified to teach others.

(2 Timothy 2:1-2)

1. What are two benefits of growing in a group instead of in isolation?

accountability
support

You might have written words such as *support*, *encouragement*, or even *accountability*. There are numerous advantages to growing as a group, but if a group is not intentional about building relationships, it is just another class.

Jesus went up on a mountainside and called to him those he wanted, and they came to him. He appointed twelve—designating them apostles—that they might be with him and that he might send them out to preach and to have authority to drive out demons. These are the twelve he appointed: Simon (to whom he gave the name Peter); James son of Zebedee and his brother John (to them he gave the name Boanerges, which means Sons of Thunder); Andrew, Philip, Bartholomew, Matthew, Thomas, James son of Alphaeus, Thaddaeus, Simon the Zealot and Judas Iscariot, who betrayed him.

(Mark 3:13-19)

They came to Capernaum. When he was in the house, he asked them, "What were you arguing about on the road?" But they kept quiet because on the way they had argued about who was the greatest.

Sitting down, Jesus called the Twelve and said, "If anyone wants to be first, he must be the very last, and the servant of all."

He took a little child and had him stand among them. Taking him in his arms, he said to them, "Whoever welcomes one of these little children in my name welcomes me; and whoever welcomes me does not welcome me but the one who sent me."

(Mark 9:33-37)

They were on their way up to Jerusalem, with Jesus leading the way, and the disciples were astonished, while those who followed were afraid. Again he took the Twelve aside and told them what was going to happen to him. "We are going up to Jerusalem," he said, "and the Son of Man will be betrayed to the chief priests and teachers of the law. They will condemn him to death and will hand him over to the Gentiles, who will mock him and spit on him, flog him and kill him. Three days later he will rise."

(Mark 10:32-34)

God Is Relational

Jesus modeled relationship with His disciples.

2. Read the following passages in the margin to see Jesus' model: Mark 3:13-19; 9:33-37; 10:32-34.

- How many people were in Jesus' discipleship group?

  12

- Why wasn't the group open to anyone who wanted to show up?

  accountability / mangeability

- How did Jesus give special attention to this group?

Jesus' group of twelve men was not open for people to come and go as they pleased. At times, He did set them apart for special discussions, teaching, and relationship.

Are You Relational?

If you are working through this manual as intended, you have been meeting in a small group for five or six weeks. Your discussions have likely ranged from theology to sports and from family to work.

3. See if you can answer the following questions about four people in your group without their help.

Name	His or Her Story
	Where they work: _____
	Spouse or girl/boyfriend: _____
	Children's names: _____
	Where they grew up: _____
	Favorite hobby: _____
	Where they work: _____
	Spouse or girl/boyfriend: _____
	Children's names: _____
	Where they grew up: _____
	Favorite hobby: _____

Name	His or Her Story
	Where they work: _____ Spouse or girl/boyfriend: _____ Children's names: _____ Where they grew up: _____ Favorite hobby: _____
	Where they work: _____ Spouse or girl/boyfriend: _____ Children's names: _____ Where they grew up: _____ Favorite hobby: _____

How well do you know the people in your group? Your answers indicate the depth of your relationships.

4. Place an "X" on the line below representing how well you know your group on average.

●——●

Don't have a clue   Acquaintances   Know some   Know them well —
                                            about them   their strengths and
                                                              weaknesses

If you did well in filling out the above list, you already know the value of being relational. If you weren't able to fill in the list, take some time this week to hear a little of each other's stories.

An intentional leader can guide and strengthen a small group's relational environment by encouraging people to share about their lives. Simple questions about families, experiences, hopes, and fears provide relational opportunities. If the group size does not allow enough time for each person to be heard, then it is too big.

If you are the leader of a small group, you can intentionally help the members of your group to share their stories with each other. You already have a tool in the list above.

5. List three questions you might use to build relationships in a group:

● _____
_____
_____

● _____
_____
_____

● _____
_____
_____

A good place to start is past, present, and future. For example:

- **Past**: What is your fondest childhood memory?
- **Present**: Are you where you thought you would be ten years ago?
- **Future**: If you had one wish for your future, what would it be?

Remember, it is not only your job to create a relational environment; each member of your group contributes to relational health and depth. Deep relationships don't happen accidentally and are essential for discipleship.

Review

- A relational environment is more than a class or group. It requires people to share their lives.
- God is relational by nature; Jesus and Paul modeled relational environments. Therefore, discipleship happens best in a relational environment.

OPENING RELATIONSHIPS SO DISCIPLES CAN GROW

day 2

Many of us have been hurt by people who shared embarrassing things about us with others; however, today we challenge you to open your life to people.

Here are three elements of a relational environment in a small group:

- A relational environment is characterized by authenticity.
- A relational environment includes mutual accountability.
- An intentional leader creates a safe relational environment.

Authentic Relationships

Adults hide their fears, struggles, hurts, and their questions, even while they are sitting in a small group. Hiding creates pretend relationships, not authentic ones. Honesty creates trust. When people are honest with us and "tell it like it is," it encourages us to be honest with them.

1. Read 1 John 1:6-7 in the margin and complete this sentence:

> The first key to authentic relationships is seeing that how we relate
> to ____God____ affects how we relate to _____
> ___people___.

If we say that we have fellowship with Him and yet walk in the darkness, we lie and do not practice the truth; but if we walk in the Light as He Himself is in the Light, we have fellowship with one another, and the blood of Jesus His Son cleanses us from all sin.

(1 John 1:6-7, NASB)

The correct answers are *God* and *each other*.

Hiding from God puts barriers between Him and us. Authentic fellowship starts with being open with God. After all, He already knows all about us, and can even see us in the dark (see Psalm 139:12). But God is light, and we are to walk with God as Jesus walks with Him: in the light.

The second key to authentic relationships is walking in the light together. The word *walk* is another way of saying how we live—how we conduct ourselves every day.

2. Look back at 1 John 1:7 in the margin. What do you think "walk in the Light" means? Check the best descriptions:

- ☐ Being polite to people you resent
- ☐ Living out God's character as best you can
- ☐ Speaking truth motivated by love rather than judging others
- ☐ Forgiving others—keeping short accounts
- ☐ Keeping quiet when people hurt you and suffering in silence
- ☐ Building relationships with only people who share your preferences

Secure relationships help people to stop hiding their struggles. Items 2, 3, and 4 characterize walking in the light. It is easier to walk in the light with God than with our brothers and sisters, yet He tells us to be authentic and tell others our sins and failures.

He who conceals his sins does not prosper, but whoever confesses and renounces them finds mercy.
(Proverbs 28:13)

Confess your sins to one another, and pray for one another so that you may be healed. The effective prayer of a righteous man can accomplish much.
(James 5:16, NASB)

Even if anyone is caught in any trespass, you who are spiritual, restore such a one in a spirit of gentleness; each one looking to yourself, so that you too will not be tempted. Bear one another's burdens, and thereby fulfill the law of Christ.
(Galatians 6:1-2, NASB)

3. Read the verses in the margin and write the benefits of confessing our sins:

- Proverbs 28:13

- James 5:16

- Galatians 6:1-2

If we walk in the light with people as Jesus walks in the light with the Father, we will find compassion. We will be healed and others will share our burdens.

4. Write the correct word in the following blank:

A relational environment is characterized by ____transparency____.

A relational environment includes mutual accountability.

An intentional leader creates a safe relational environment.

Accountability and Encouragement

Sharing our struggles is only the starting place for growth; we need accountability to mature. A leader creates this relational environment intentionally by appropriately sharing personal struggles and victories with the group. That transparency encourages other people to stop hiding. As disciple-makers, we need people to hold us accountable to do the right thing, to share our burdens when we fail, and to encourage us. Authenticity and accountability are necessary for growth. It's difficult—if not impossible—to grow spiritually without both.

A disciple-maker leads the group to authenticity and accountability by modeling transparency. Though Jesus had no sin, He openly shared His struggles with the disciples (see John 12:27; Matthew 26:37-38; Mark 10:32-34; Luke 13:33-35). A discipleship group needs accountability, but it also needs other important components. Modeling, shepherding, real teaching and learning, as well as service all combine to make a disciple. As disciple-makers share, it is always important that the focus is on Christ, especially His forgiveness and help.

5. What do you think might hinder you from being transparent in a disciple-making group?

_____

_____

_____

6. What can you do to overcome those fears and obstacles?

_____

_____

_____

7. Write in the blanks two essentials for creating a relational environment.

A relational environment is characterized by _____.

A relational environment includes _____ _____.

An intentional leader creates a safe relational environment.

Safe Environment

When you are authentic and walk in the light with God, those you disciple experience a safe environment where they can follow your model. As an intentional leader, you help create this environment by showing the traits listed in Proverbs 28:13, James 5:16, and Galatians 6:1-2.

8. Read the three Scriptures again. This time write what creates a safe environment:

_____

_____

_____

The things that help create a safe environment are compassion, praying for one another, a spirit of gentleness, an awareness of your own vulnerability, restoration of those caught in sin, and bearing one another's burdens.

Review

- Write in the blanks three essentials for creating a relational environment.

A relational environment is characterized by _____.

A relational environment includes _____ _____.

An intentional leader creates __ _____ _____ _____.

day 3   REAL TEACHING, REAL LEARNING

Creating a relational environment paves the way for learning about God and His Word. Today we talk specifically about how people learn best in a small group. A teacher cannot respond well to the individual learning needs of a student if the class is large.

Following are three ways that large class size affects learning.

1. For each sentence, fill in the blank with the word—*lecture, time,* or *include*—that completes it.

    If the class is large, there will not be enough _____ to answer all of the students' questions.

    In a large class, it becomes difficult to _____ everyone in a discussion.

    Large classes force teachers to use _____ as their primary method for communicating.

Most of us do not choose lecture as a preferred way to learn, but unfortunately the lecture model is how most Christians receive much of their teaching. Jesus did preach to large crowds, but He did not use the lecture model to make disciples.

2. Take a minute and think about how Jesus trained His disciples. List four different methods you remember of how He taught them.

    - _____
    - _____
    - _____
    - _____

We have already mentioned that Jesus taught in small groups. Your list might also include methods such as storying, on-the-job training, question-and-answer, and modeling. We want to emphasize three methods in today's lesson: modeling, telling Bible stories, and healthy dialogue through questions and answers.

Modeling

The disciples witnessed Jesus' deep, abiding relationship with His Father. They walked beside Him as He pursued lost, hurting people. They felt the warm acceptance of His love for them. As disciples, they did their best to imitate Jesus, just as we do. As disciple-makers, we do all we can to let those we disciple see how we follow Him.

3. Read the three passages in the margin. For each characteristic that Jesus modeled and that we are to imitate, write the corresponding Scripture reference.

_____ A longing for lost people to be saved
_____ A deep love for our brothers and sisters in Christ
_____ A desire for God to be glorified

Your answers should be in the following order: Romans 9:1-3; 1 Peter 1:22-23; 2 Corinthians 4:5,16-18.

Telling Bible Stories

Jesus told stories to teach God's truth.

4. The questions on the left were ones that were asked of Jesus. Read the Scripture in your Bible, and then write why you think Jesus used a story to answer the question.

"Is it lawful to heal on the Sabbath?" Matthew 12:9-13	
"Lord, how many times shall I forgive my brother when he sins against me? Up to seven times?" Matthew 18:21-35	
"Who is my neighbor?" Luke 10:25-37	

His stories convicted the listeners because of their actions. They could not condemn Jesus without condemning themselves, and therefore the stories made Jesus' point better than a lecture.

We have those stories preserved for us in the Bible, so we can use them as well. In week 12, we will spend more time on Bible storying, but for now, remember that Bible storying is one of the most effective tools Jesus used.

Healthy Dialogue: Question-and-Answer

Jesus not only told stories, He asked and answered questions to help His followers apply the truth of those stories.

Our church has an ongoing partnership with several churches in Ethiopia. In Soddo, Ethiopia, daily life is filled with the steady blaring noise of religious leaders shouting over loudspeakers. Christians, Muslims, and Orthodox all use this loudspeaker method to blast their messages across the city, like "lecture on steroids." Each group believes that talking louder and longer will gather followers, but that is not how you make disciples.

It is through dialogue that disciples understand and apply the message. A group that is relationally safe lends itself to open discussion and application. An intentional leader

We do not preach ourselves, but Jesus Christ as Lord, and ourselves as your servants for Jesus' sake. . . .

Therefore we do not lose heart. Though outwardly we are wasting away, yet inwardly we are being renewed day by day. For our light and momentary troubles are achieving for us an eternal glory that far outweighs them all. So we fix our eyes not on what is seen, but on what is unseen. For what is seen is temporary, but what is unseen is eternal.

(2 Corinthians 4:5,16-18)

I speak the truth in Christ—I am not lying, my conscience confirms it in the Holy Spirit—I have great sorrow and unceasing anguish in my heart. For I could wish that I myself were cursed and cut off from Christ for the sake of my brothers, those of my own race.

(Romans 9:1-3)

Now that you have purified yourselves by obeying the truth so that you have sincere love for your brothers, love one another deeply, from the heart. For you have been born again, not of perishable seed, but of imperishable, through the living and enduring word of God.

(1 Peter 1:22-23)

helps disciples engage God's Word through the give and take of dialogue, asking and answering questions like Jesus did. Sound Bible teaching and learning are essential food for a disciple's growth, but you are not making disciples if you are doing all the talking.

A Real Life Ministries Story

Desalegn is a dedicated Christian leader in the Ethiopian church. Three years ago, he became a member of a relationally based discipleship group. Each week the leader came with a story from God's Word, and he also shared his own life story. Gradually, relationships in the group became safe and strong. They began to focus on real-life issues. The leader's questions drew the group to apply Bible stories to their own lives.

Through this small group, Desalegn acquired the tools to make disciples. He leads several groups on his own now and is raising up new disciple-makers. His enthusiasm for the mission of Christ is contagious. God's Word has come alive in these small groups, and people are experiencing real change. Though he has been a Christian for a long time, Desalegn has now become an intentional disciple-maker.

5. Match the disciple's need with the disciple-maker's role:

Disciple's Need	Disciple-Maker's Role
A. I need to see how a disciple lives.	___ Healthy dialogue
B. I need biblical truth that is memorable and applicable.	___ Bible storying
C. I have questions about the Bible.	___ Modeling

The correct answers are C, B, and A.

Review

In a relational environment for discipleship, small-group leaders use these three methods of teaching:

- Modeling—they demonstrate the life of a disciple
- Bible stories—they use Bible storying to apply biblical truth
- Healthy dialogue—they answer people's questions from the Bible

SHEPHERDING DISCIPLES

day 4

As our church has grown, we have found that certain values mark effective small groups. Today we look at one of the most critical values: shepherding. At a pastors' conference, Jim Putman was teased because he spent every Monday calling people who were missing at church. Jim's commitment to calling the missing people came from Ezekiel 34.

God describes the essence of a relational environment throughout the Bible in the terms of a shepherd tending his sheep. Read Ezekiel 34:2-5 in the margin. In this passage, the shepherds of Israel are rebuked for their lack of care for the people.

1. The Bible uses sheep to make this point, but people are not livestock. Match the positive acts of shepherding from Ezekiel 34:4-5 with a practical application of what it looks like to shepherd people.

Son of man, prophesy against the shepherds of Israel; prophesy and say to them: "This is what the Sovereign LORD says: Woe to the shepherds of Israel who only take care of themselves! Should not shepherds take care of the flock? You eat the curds, clothe yourselves with the wool and slaughter the choice animals, but you do not take care of the flock. You have not strengthened the weak or healed the sick or bound up the injured. You have not brought back the strays or searched for the lost. You have ruled them harshly and brutally. So they were scattered because there was no shepherd, and when they were scattered they became food for all the wild animals."

(Ezekiel 34:2-5)

___ Strengthened the weak	A. For those who have been missing for a few weeks, we could give them a call or visit them and let them know they are missed.
___ Healed the sick	B. For those absent from the group due to illness, we could pray for them, take them to the doctor, and take a meal over to their house.
___ Bound up the injured	C. For those overwhelmed with life and starting to fail, I could spend time with them reminding them of the ways God had provided for them in the past.
___ Brought back strays	D. Our leadership should be firm but fair, executed with an attitude of kindness and love.
___ Searched for the lost	E. For those hurt or wounded by others, we could all write encouragement cards to them assuring them of our prayers and support.
___ You should not rule them harshly and brutally	F. If someone has left the group and is moving away from Christ, we could take another person with us and go visit.

2. Which of these acts of shepherding have you experienced in a small group? Circle the corresponding letters.

3. Which have you wanted to experience but have not? Draw a triangle around the corresponding letters.

The practical application of Ezekiel 34:4-5 for the list above is in this order: C, B, E, F, A, and D.

Share the Shepherding

Christ is the primary Shepherd of His people (see 1 Peter 5:4). Our role as leaders is to cooperate with Christ in providing a relational environment that facilitates shepherding, both through our efforts and through the efforts of others in the group.

4. Which of the following are benefits that group members receive personally when they show concern for members outside of the weekly meeting? Underline the correct answers.

    A. They feel a deeper sense of ownership for the group.
    B. They have more time for themselves.
    C. They experience God working through them.
    D. They move closer to seeing themselves as disciple-makers.
    E. They overcome fears of relational risk.

The only answer that should *not* be underlined is B. Healthy relationships require time. God uses these relationships to grow disciples.

Value, Not an Obligation

It is easy to slip into a mindset of feeling burdened by obligation, even in shepherding. When this happens, we risk losing the joy of making disciples. At our church, we have a computer program that helps us keep track of people so they won't slip through the cracks. Last year, after training a new leader on this program, the individual made an interesting comment: "All this time I thought my leader called me to see how I was doing. Now I know that he was completing his calls to enter in on the computer." Uh-oh! We must never let the tool we use replace the value we created it for in the first place: shepherding our people.

5. What could you do to keep your heart right about shepherding the people in your group?

....
....
....
....

One final note on Ezekiel: The shepherds were rebuked because they had not brought back the strays or searched for the lost. Sheep stray. People become hurt, tempted, or distracted and wander off. Intentional leaders care about people enough to go after them.

6. Indicate where your efforts rank in bringing back the strays by placing an "X" on the line in the appropriate place for each statement.

"I contact people when they miss a small-group meeting."

●━━━━━━━━━━━━━━━━━━━━━━━━━━━━━━━━━━━━━━●

Not at all   Sometimes   Every week

"I contact small-group members when I notice they have missed Sunday worship service."

Not at all   Sometimes   Every week

"I contact small-group members when I discover they are going through a difficult circumstance."

Not at all   Sometimes   Every week

"I contact small-group members when I learn they have a problem with me or another member of the small group."

Not at all   Sometimes   Every week

In order to create an effective relational environment, intentional leaders need to be shepherds who guide small-group members into caring for one another. We model what playing together as a team looks like, and we help prepare each person to play his or her part. We come alongside to coach people when they stumble and fall. Finally, we go after people when they stray or lose their way.

Review
- The leader of a discipling small group has a responsibility to shepherd members of the group.
- Shepherding is the job of everyone in the group.
- If shepherding is not a value, it hinders the group from making healthy disciples.

day 5

SHEPHERDING EACH OTHER

One of our church members was admitted to the hospital, and Jim Putman went to visit her. In the waiting room, he was greeted by several small-group members who had arrived ahead of him. When he got up to the room, people were already there, praying, encouraging, and meeting the family's needs during this crisis.

Out in the hallway, the nurse in charge was surprised and mildly flustered. Jim asked if there was something he could do. She responded, "Who are all these people? They can't all be family."

"Well," Jim responded, "they are and they aren't. You see, these are people from your patient's small group at our church. They think they *are* family."

They devoted themselves to the apostles' teaching and to the fellowship, to the breaking of bread and to prayer. Everyone was filled with awe, and many wonders and miraculous signs were done by the apostles. All the believers were together and had everything in common. Selling their possessions and goods, they gave to anyone as he had need. Every day they continued to meet together in the temple courts. They broke bread in their homes and ate together with glad and sincere hearts, praising God and enjoying the favor of all the people. And the Lord added to their number daily those who were being saved. . . .

All the believers were one in heart and mind. No one claimed that any of his possessions was his own, but they shared everything they had. With great power the apostles continued to testify to the resurrection of the Lord Jesus, and much grace was upon them all. There were no needy persons among them. For from time to time those who owned lands or houses sold them, brought the money from the sales and put it at the apostles' feet, and it was distributed to anyone as he had need.

(Acts 2:42-47; 4:32-35)

1. How would you feel if you were in the hospital and your small group did this for you?

_____

_____

_____

_____

2. What would you think about the relationships in that small group if you were the nurse?

_____

_____

_____

_____

Meeting Physical Needs

If you were in the hospital, you would likely be pleased to know that your small group cared for you. But this small group's response impacted the nurse, too. Rarely had she seen people whose relationships were that strong. Small groups with a relational environment provide more than a meeting time for discipleship. Likewise, the shepherding that takes place in a relational environment extends beyond the four walls of the meeting place. It is more than noticing who is absent on small-group night.

3. Read Acts 2:42-47 and 4:32-35 in the margin. Circle words from this list that describe the relationships of the first discipleship groups.

Distant	Caring	Sharing	Isolated
Giving	Meeting Needs	Surface	Lonely
Together	Unified	Grace-Filled	Judgmental

4. Look at Acts 2:47 again. What impact were the relationships in the church having on others outside?

Words such as *caring*, *grace-filled*, and *unified* certainly describe the relational environment of the early church. However, it is important to notice that those relationships spilled out of the group and onto others, causing the church to gain favor with other people as well.

The "Spillover" Result

When Janet moved, her neighbor asked her where she had found so much help. Janet is a widow in our community, and her family lives in another state. On moving day, twenty people with trucks and smiles converged on her house and stayed until every last possession had been transported to her new home. Most of them were people from her small group. Her neighbors were impressed. They had assumed that Janet's circle of close friends was small, but it was not.

A relational environment meets spiritual needs, but it also meets physical needs as well. That was part of what attracted others to the disciples in the book of Acts. People outside of the church witnessed a caring community that did more than talk. They shared their possessions, time, and energy in meeting the needs of each other. A disciple-maker understands this key biblical and relational principle. He or she leads growing disciples to serve each other in tangible ways. The spillover result is often other people who become interested in following Jesus.

Loving with Our Actions

5. Read 1 John 3:16-19 in the margin and complete the following sentences so that they agree with John's words.

The love of Jesus was proven to be real by His _____.

Because Jesus gave His life up for us we should _____.

True disciples not only say they love others, they _____.

Your answers should have come directly from the verses. The love of Jesus is made known by His disciples when they give of themselves for each other. This love is not a program, a class, or a checklist; it is the very nature of a relational environment.

Recently, a family in our church took a meal over to a couple that had just had their first baby. The new mother exclaimed, "We really can't take any more food. The refrigerator is full." Her small group had provided meals almost every night, and the leftovers were piling up. Such abundance of "met needs" is a common occurrence in our small groups. When an intentional leader builds a relational environment, the love of God shows itself in many ways.

This is how we know what love is: Jesus Christ laid down his life for us. And we ought to lay down our lives for our brothers. If anyone has material possessions and sees his brother in need but has no pity on him, how can the love of God be in him? Dear children, let us not love with words or tongue but with actions and in truth. This then is how we know that we belong to the truth, and how we set our hearts at rest in his presence.

(1 John 3:16-19)

Let's use the following quiz to review what we've learned in all of week 6.

1. Disciples are made best in a _____ group.

    a. small
    b. large
    c. midsize

2. God is relational by nature; therefore, discipleship requires a _____ environment.

    a. fun
    b. relational
    c. serious

3. _____ is the responsibility of the disciple-maker, and it is the job of everyone in the group.

    a. Providing snacks
    b. Prayer
    c. Shepherding

4. Three kinds of effective teaching in a discipleship group are modeling, healthy dialogue, and telling _____ _____.

    a. engaging lecture
    b. test answers
    c. Bible stories

5. A relational environment is characterized by authenticity and _____.

    a. friendship
    b. accountability
    c. independence

6. An intentional leader helps create a relational environment by being _____.

    a. prepared
    b. transparent
    c. punctual

7. The relational environment produces acts of _____ that flow over to other people.

    a. courage
    b. service
    c. struggle

Answers: 1. a, 2. b, 3. c, 4. c, 5. b, 6. b, 7. b

Review

- A relational environment meets people's physical needs.
- When disciples meet needs, that service flows onto others as well.
- Putting love into action is proof that we are followers of Jesus.

a closer look at the reproducible process

Remember the wheel used in week 3 to explain the stages of spiritual growth? Take a minute to review it here.

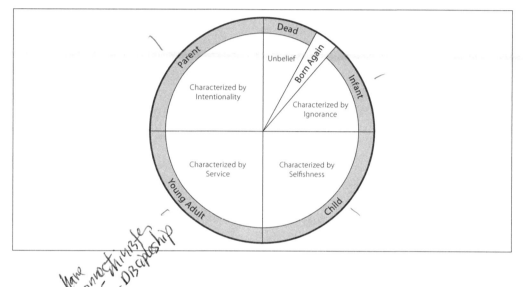

THE SCMD PROCESS

This week is an overview of how the reproducible process cooperates with the stages of growth. On the following wheel diagram find the ring near the center of the wheel. It contains the stages of spiritual growth.

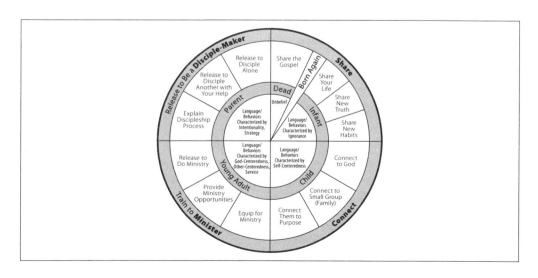

1. Write the words from the outer ring of the wheel diagram that match up with the stages of spiritual growth.

Stage of Spiritual Growth		Word from Outer Ring
Spiritually Dead	←→	*share*
Infant	←→	*Connect*
Child	←→	
Young Adult	←→	*trained*
Parent	←→	*released*

A Real Life Ministries Story

Brandon Guindon was teaching a team of church planters how the SCMD process worked to make disciples in small groups. There he met Jimmy, a man in his early twenties. Jimmy was funny, relational, and just a great guy.

At first Jimmy was disengaged and looked bored. He had grown up in the church, but in his college years he had walked away from the Lord. As the training continued, Jimmy began to engage more, even answering questions Brandon posed to the group.

During lunch on the second day of the training, Jimmy sat quietly, arms crossed with a frustrated look on his face. When Brandon asked what was on his mind, Jimmy blurted out, "I never knew any of this stuff! I grew up in the church and never ever was taught about being a disciple. I sat in church every Sunday, listened to sermons, and even attended Sunday school classes. I had no idea there was any kind of intentional process. My mom did her best, but she had no clue how to be intentional. I want to be discipled by someone!"

For the first time, Jimmy saw what could be. He saw that Jesus had an intentional process to make disciples, and he wanted it more than ever in his life.

2. Do you know people like Jimmy? Write their names here.

_____

_____

_____

_____

You may have written your own name. Did you? Could you learn more of what Jimmy saw that day—a process to disciple people?

The SCMD Process

As we mentioned earlier, at Real Life we use the concepts of **share**, **connect**, **minister**, and **disciple** (SCMD) to provide a common language for the discipleship process. Jesus intentionally met people where they were at in their growth. The SCMD process comes out of His example. This process helps people think in terms of what to *do*, not just what to *know*. This process helps disciple-makers be intentional as they lead others through the stages of spiritual growth.

Here is an overview of how we bring a person through the SCMD process. Fill in the blanks after each paragraph.

Share: At the beginning of the discipleship process, we intentionally share the gospel, its truth, and our lives with those who are spiritually dead. We purposely look for such opportunities. With those who are spiritual infants, we share what it means to follow Christ as His disciple.

3. A disciple-maker **shares** with those who are spiritually _____ as well as with spiritual _____.

Connect: As people begin to grow in their faith, an intentional disciple-maker helps them connect to God, to others, and to their purpose in the church. This connect-level discipleship happens primarily with a spiritual child, who knows about Christ but has never grown in relationship with Him and His followers. At this level, the intentional disciple-maker emphasizes the relational nature of discipleship.

4. A disciple-maker helps spiritual _____ **connect** relationally with God and other disciples.

Minister: In the third step of the process, the disciple is maturing and becoming a spiritual young adult. The intentional disciple-maker trains spiritual young adults to use their gifts and abilities to minister to others. Disciple-makers equip, encourage, and walk with these young adults as they do ministry.

5. A disciple-maker equips and encourages spiritual _____ _____ as they **minister**.

Disciple: In the fourth stage, disciples are becoming spiritual parents and are accepting the responsibility to intentionally disciple others. An intentional disciple-maker equips and releases his or her disciple to disciple others—to be spiritual parents for other disciples. During this stage, we become peers with those we have discipled. We now support each other to make disciples.

6. Finally, a disciple-maker releases a spiritual _____ to intentionally **disciple** others.

7. Let's see if you can apply these descriptions in the following statements. Place an S, C, M, or D next to the statement that best fits what you as an intentional leader need to do.

_____M_____ I have noticed that my disciple is ready to start leading a group for the first time and helping other people.

_____S_____ I realize that my neighbor does not believe in Christ, so I need to look for opportunities to present the gospel.

_____D_____ The person I have been discipling is beginning to disciple other people. I need to release and equip him to do this on his own.

_____C_____ I just met a new person in our church. She is eager to join a small group, so I am going to invite her to join ours this week.

How did you do? Your answers should be: M, S, D, C. Remember that each step in the SCMD process requires intentional action from the leader to help the disciple move toward the next stage.

8. As you look at the overview of the reproducible process, how intentional have you been as a disciple-maker? Check the answer that best fits you.

☐ I am like Jimmy in the opening story. I am just learning there is an intentional process that can be reproduced.

☐ I have tried to help people grow, but I didn't have a clear plan for helping them become disciples who make disciples.

☐ I have generally done what I could to help people, but I have not known how to help them grow and reproduce.

☐ I intentionally help people grow and reproduce and can show others how to as well.

Review

- There is a reproducible process of spiritual growth: share, connect, minister, and disciple.
- Each step corresponds to stages of disciple growth.
- One must be intentional to help disciples grow to reproduce.

JESUS MODELED SHARING

day 2

The rest of this week, we will provide you with an overview of the reproducible process (SCMD). If it seems as if we are racing through the material, don't worry. We spend a week on each phase of the process in weeks 8 through 11. In order for something to be intentional, it must be reproducible. If it is going to be reproducible, it must be understood.

Sharing with the Spiritually Dead

Jesus, the greatest disciple-maker, is our model for how the process of discipleship begins. How did Jesus share His life and message with those who were spiritually dead?

1. We see an example of how He shared in John 4:4-42, the story of the woman at the well. Take a moment to read the story in your Bible. Then circle each of the ways Jesus shared with her.

    A. He waited until the woman spoke to Him first.
    B. He asked a leading question to peak her interest. ✓
    C. He disregarded social prejudice so He could relate to her. ✓
    D. He cared primarily about His own thirst.
    E. He began by quoting a lot of Scripture to her.
    F. He was sensitive to her spiritual need. ✓
    G. He was careful not to condemn her for the lifestyle of a spiritually dead person. ✓
    H. He was quick to win an argument with her.

    You should have circled B, C, F, and G.

    At the beginning of the story, the Samaritan woman was spiritually dead. Jesus met her as she was. As God in the flesh, He knew all about her and her struggles, yet He did not walk up to her and condemn her for her sin or pronounce judgment on her. Instead, He began a conversation with her. He spent time with her, just as He had done with the disciples on the shores of Galilee. He went to where she lived, got into her world, and interacted with her in a relationship. He didn't lecture her or enter into a debate with her.

    He shared the gospel with her in a way she could understand, describing salvation as "living water" (verses 10 and 13). He was not stopped by her gender, her morality, or her ethnicity. He created a desire in her for the gospel by telling the difference in the water she sought and the water He gave. Once He had her attention, He began to share the gospel—the good news—with her. (Next week we will show you a simple plan for explaining the gospel to someone.)

2. Which of the following obstacles hinder you from sharing with spiritually dead people?

    ☐ Discomfort with people's lifestyle
    ☐ Fear of not knowing answers to people's questions
    ☑ Fear of being criticized or rejected
    ☑ Not knowing what to say

☐ Not having access to non-Christians
☐ Feeling too overwhelmed and busy to take on another thing

3. How can you be more like Jesus and intentionally share with a spiritually dead person?

Be prepared to share your answers with your small group.

Sharing with Spiritual Infants

Jesus did not stop at the gospel. Once the woman accepted the truth about who He was, she believed in Him (see verses 28-29). Even though He was on His way to Galilee, Jesus did not abandon the woman or the other new believers in town. He spent two days with them. Of course, we do not have a complete record of what transpired during that time, but because of how Jesus discipled other people, we can assume that He continued to disciple the people of Sychar. When we spend time with spiritual infants, we help them understand truth and form new habits.

Read this list of new habits we should help spiritual infants develop:

- Regular Bible reading
- Church attendance
- Prayer
- Tithing
- Commitment to a small group

They also need our support and help for losing any bad habits they may have.

4. List other habits that you think spiritual infants may need to develop:

Scrip memory

Be prepared to share your answers with your small group.

Review
- We are to share with spiritually dead people and infant believers.
- We should share our lives, the gospel, truth, and new habits.

JESUS MODELED CONNECTING

day 3

Today we look at relationships and their importance in helping spiritual infants move to the next stage of growth. We use the word *connect* to illustrate the bond that Christians share with each other as members of God's family. We also rely on the word *connect* to underscore the necessity of discipleship being done in the context of relationship. Disciple-making is not simply a transfer of information.

Individualism Versus Others

Many Christians have bought into the idea that they can do Christianity by themselves, without other people. They think they can sit alone on the lake, in the woods, or even at home and relate to God with no need for relationship with other disciples. While they try to stay connected to God, they ignore His design to be connected to others. Meanwhile, they are dying on the inside because no one truly knows them, and seemingly no one cares. Worse yet, they are not growing as disciples and are unable to fulfill Christ's command (see Matthew 28:18-20).

We think this belief system contradicts Jesus' words in Mark 12:29-31.

1. Read Mark 12:29-31 in the margin and answer the following questions:

   * What is the relationship described in the first commandment?

     love for God

   * What relationship is described in the second commandment?

     love for neighbor

   * How would Jesus' words conflict with the belief that "I can do Christianity by myself"?

"The most important one," answered Jesus, *"is this: 'Hear, O Israel, the Lord our God, the Lord is one. Love the Lord your God with all your heart and with all your soul and with all your mind and with all your strength.' The second is this: 'Love your neighbor as yourself.' There is no commandment greater than these."*
(Mark 12:29-31)

Jesus indicated that to completely fulfill God's commands you need two categories of relationships. First, you must be in relationship (connected) with God. Second, you will be in relationship (connected) with your neighbor. Both of these connections are vital.

Connecting with God

Jesus modeled a deep, abiding relationship with God the Father. The disciples observed Jesus' relationship with God in daily life as well as in a time of distress.

"Why were you searching for me?" he asked. "Didn't you know I had to be in my Father's house?"
(Luke 2:49)

To those who sold doves he said, "Get these out of here! How dare you turn my Father's house into a market!"
(John 2:16)

Jesus said, "I praise you, Father, Lord of heaven and earth, because you have hidden these things from the wise and learned, and revealed them to little children. Yes, Father, for this was your good pleasure.
"All things have been committed to me by my Father. No one knows the Son except the Father, and no one knows the Father except the Son and those to whom the Son chooses to reveal him."
(Matthew 11:25-27)

For this reason the Jews tried all the harder to kill him; not only was he breaking the Sabbath, but he was even calling God his own Father, making himself equal with God.
Jesus gave them this answer: "I tell you the truth, the Son can do nothing by himself; he can do only what he sees his Father doing, because whatever the Father does the Son also does. For the Father loves the Son and shows him all he does. Yes, to your amazement he will show him even greater things than these."
(John 5:18-20)

2. Read the following passages in the margin and write a phrase that describes Jesus' connection with the Father.

Luke 2:49	had to be ...
John 2:16	turn ...
Matthew 11:25-27	thanx
John 5:18-20	love connection

Your answers should be similar to the following: Even as a child, Jesus wanted to be about His Father's business (see Luke 2:49). In John 2:16, Jesus was indignant because His Father's house was being used for dishonest profit. Jesus openly spoke to the Father, expressing His gratitude and praise (see Matthew 11:25-27). In John 5:18-20, Jesus' relationship with God the Father revealed a deep, loving connection.

Jesus knew that His disciples needed a relationship with God that went beyond just surface knowledge. He spent time together with them and built a strong connection. They came into relationship with God through Jesus. He connected with His disciples in a real bond, not a distant association.

3. Let's assess your connection with God on two levels: frequency and depth. Place an "X" in the box that best describes you.

The **frequency** in which I spend time specifically with God is:

	Regularly throughout the day	At a set time each day	Once or twice a week	Hit and miss, but at least monthly
Frequency				

The **depth** of my relationship with God would be best described as:

	Like an ocean	Like a lake	Like a pond	Like a mud puddle
Depth				

We hope you are striving to become a disciple who spends time with God and in as deep a connection as possible.

Connecting Spiritual Children with a Spiritual Family

Along with connecting to God, disciples need relationships with each other. As children need a family to be healthy, spiritual children need a family in order to grow strong and healthy.

Jesus continually modeled and promoted connection with others. He didn't just meet with His disciples one-on-one for an hour a week; He also brought them into a small group of twelve to do life together. This group was inseparable for three years. The level at which Jesus' disciples connected together in a group illustrates the value Jesus placed on in-depth relationships. Though we may not be able to spend 24/7 with those we disciple, we must be in relationship with them at a deeper level than just a weekly meeting.

4. Read 1 John 4:19-21 in the margin. What does this passage say about the importance of being connected to God and how it affects our connection with others in His family?

_____

_____

_____

_____

We love because he first loved us. If anyone says, "I love God," yet hates his brother, he is a liar. For anyone who does not love his brother, whom he has seen, cannot love God, whom he has not seen. And he has given us this command: Whoever loves God must also love his brother.
(1 John 4:19-21)

Notice what happens if we do not love each other. If we don't love fellow believers, we cannot love God. Jesus prayed for this relational connection when He said, "May they be brought to complete unity to let the world know that you sent me" (John 17:23).

The Early Disciples

We also see connection in the early church. We will look at this more in depth in week 9, but for now, read Colossians 3:12-17 in the margin.

5. Put the following phrases from these verses into your own words.

- Bear with one another

_____

_____

_____

- Together in perfect unity

_____

_____

_____

- Teach and admonish one another with all wisdom

_____

_____

_____

Therefore, as God's chosen people, holy and dearly loved, clothe yourselves with compassion, kindness, humility, gentleness and patience. Bear with each other and forgive whatever grievances you may have against one another. Forgive as the Lord forgave you. And over all these virtues put on love, which binds them all together in perfect unity.

Let the peace of Christ rule in your hearts, since as members of one body you were called to peace. And be thankful. Let the word of Christ dwell in you richly as you teach and admonish one another with all wisdom, and as you sing psalms, hymns and spiritual songs with gratitude in your hearts to God. And whatever you do, whether in word or deed, do it all in the name of the Lord Jesus, giving thanks to God the Father through him.

(Colossians 3:12-17)

6. Next write an accurate definition of the discipleship connection.
   Disciples connected in relationship means . . .

   _____

   _____

   _____

   _____

   Be prepared to share your answers with the group.

Review

- Spiritual children need to be connected in relationships with God and with other disciples.
- Jesus modeled both of these types of connection.

JESUS MODELED TRAINING FOR MINISTRY   **day 4**

It has been a few weeks since we reviewed our definition of a disciple. Can you remember the three key parts?

1. Fill in the blanks with words from this box:

mission	committed
following	changed

- A disciple is one who is _____*Following*_____ Jesus.
- A disciple is one who is being _____*changed*_____ by Jesus.
- A disciple is one who is _____*com*_____ to the ___*mission*___ of Jesus.

Go back in the book and check if you are unsure of your answers.

From the beginning, Jesus told the disciples that He would make them into something different: "Come, follow me, . . . and I will *make* you fishers of men" (Matthew 4:19, emphasis added). Their occupation of catching fish changed into a mission of fishing for people. Each step along the way, Jesus taught them to share with others, connect people to God, and minister to those who were in need. Today we look at how Jesus involved His disciples in ministry.

The Ministry Phase and Spiritual Young Adults

The ministry phase of the discipleship process matches up well with the characteristics of the young adult stage of spiritual growth, as reflected in the following table.

Young Adult Stage	Ministry Phase
Heart change from self to others God-centered in motivation Others' needs are important Desire to serve and lead	Equip for ministry/serving Provide opportunities to minister/serve Release to do ministry independently

When a disciple matures into a spiritual young adult, he or she needs training and opportunities to serve.

Hands-On Training

Jesus used everyday opportunities to train the disciples to minister. We have looked at the feeding of the five thousand to see how Jesus was an intentional leader. Let's go back to this account to discover the **ministry** phase of the disciple-making process.

Jesus crossed to the far shore of the Sea of Galilee (that is, the Sea of Tiberias), and a great crowd of people followed him because they saw the miraculous signs he had performed on the sick. Then Jesus went up on a mountainside and sat down with his disciples. The Jewish Passover Feast was near.

When Jesus looked up and saw a great crowd coming toward him, he said to Philip, "Where shall we buy bread for these people to eat?" He asked this only to test him, for he already had in mind what he was going to do.

Philip answered him, "Eight months' wages would not buy enough bread for each one to have a bite!"

Another of his disciples, Andrew, Simon Peter's brother, spoke up, "Here is a boy with five small barley loaves and two small fish, but how far will they go among so many?"

Jesus said, "Have the people sit down." There was plenty of grass in that place, and the men sat down, about five thousand of them. Jesus then took the loaves, gave thanks, and distributed to those who were seated as much as they wanted. He did the same with the fish.

When they had all had enough to eat, he said to his disciples, "Gather the pieces that are left over. Let nothing be wasted." So they gathered them and filled twelve baskets with the pieces of the five barley loaves left over by those who had eaten.

(John 6:1-13)

2. Take a moment to read John 6:1-13 in the margin. List all the things you see that Jesus had His disciples do to minister to the people.

_____

_____

_____

_____

_____

The twelve disciples served the people that day while they were learning a great lesson about who Jesus really was. They organized the groups, distributed food, and gathered up leftovers. Ministry was part of their discipleship process.

At the feeding of the five thousand, the Twelve were learning about ministry as well as about who Jesus was.

3. Mark the ministry lessons that the Twelve should have learned from the experience:

A. Only miracle workers can be involved in ministry.
B. We are responsible for doing something about others' needs. ✓
C. We depend on God to provide for others' needs. ✓
D. We serve others to make us look important.
E. Involving disciples in ministry is part of how Jesus made disciples. ✓
F. Service has to match directly to my spiritual gifts or I can't do it.
G. I learn things through serving that would be hard to learn just by listening. ✓

Statements B, C, E, and G are correct.

Jesus modeled intentional actions in His relationships with people. He **shared** with spiritual infants, **connected** with spiritual children, and actively trained the disciples to **minister** to others.

As we see in the example of the feeding of the five thousand, Jesus gave the disciples hands-on experience in learning to care for others. Jesus got His disciples "in the game." They did not sit on the outside watching Him meet all the needs of people. Jesus valued their involvement and used it for their growth as disciples. We think Jesus used this opportunity to train them and give them a process of how they should train other disciples in the future. As disciple-makers, we can utilize this process to help people grow intentionally.

4. How were you introduced to service/ministry?

_____

_____

_____

_____

_____

5. Answer the following questions about the process you experienced by circling Yes (Y) or No (N):

Y   N   Were you well equipped to serve before you were on your own?
Y   N   Were you given opportunities to serve and then coached as you went?
Y   N   Were you asked about your heart for God before you were asked to serve?
Y   N   Did your service stem from an attitude of caring for others in need?
Y   N   Were you released to serve independently before you felt ready?
Y   N   If you made a mistake, did someone take the time to help you learn from it and improve?

We tend to train others for making disciples the same way we were introduced to ministry. Think about how intentional you could be when leading someone through the **ministry** phase of discipleship.

6. Write three things you would like to remember to do in the **ministry** phase of making a disciple:

- ....
  ....
- ....
  ....
- ....
  ....

Be prepared to share your answers with your small group.

Review
- The ministry phase of the SCMD process matches up with the spiritual stage of young adult.
- Jesus intentionally involved His disciples in ministry/service to train them.

day 5   JESUS MODELED RELEASING DISCIPLES

Today we conclude our overview of the reproducible process. SCMD is our road map for moving disciples through the stages of spiritual growth. We are going to cover each aspect of this process in more depth in the coming weeks. This week we have been focused on the biblical support for this process.

1. Can you name the spiritual stage of growth that matches the phase of the SCMD process? Feel free to look back at this week's lessons if you need help.

Phase of SCMD	Stage of Spiritual Growth
SHARE	*dead / infant* *Should be two stages listed here.*
CONNECT	*child*
MINISTER	*y adult*
DISCIPLE	*adult parent*

The Disciple Phase and Spiritual Parents

Spiritual parents are ready and able to lead a person through the stages of spiritual growth, which means they are ready for the disciple phase of the process. Spiritual parents can share the gospel with people. They help them connect and get them "into the game." Spiritual parents are finally ready to learn how to cooperate with God in order to help others become disciple-makers, too.

2. Review this summary table, which matches the disciple phase with the stage of spiritual parent.

Spiritual Parent Stage	Disciple Phase
Able to reproduce Able to feed themselves Value the church team	Explain the discipleship process Release to disciple with the disciple-maker along to help Release to disciple independent of the disciple-maker

Jesus on the Disciple Phase

3. Read Matthew 28:18-20 in the margin. Which of the following did Jesus do leading up to this event in order to prepare His twelve disciples?

    A. Jesus had written a to-do list for them to follow.

    B. Jesus had put them into ministry/service of others in need.

    C. Jesus had given them real teaching.

    D. Jesus shared with them that He was the Son of God.

    E. Jesus had connected them to God and to each other.

    F. Jesus had equipped and released them to do ministry/service.

    G. Jesus had held classes once a week for them to attend.

    H. Jesus had shared truth that was new to them.

    I. Jesus had shown them disicpleship as they were together.

Jesus came to them and said, "All authority in heaven and on earth has been given to me. Therefore go and make disciples of all nations, baptizing them in the name of the Father and of the Son and of the Holy Spirit, and teaching them to obey everything I have commanded you. And surely I am with you always, to the very end of the age."

(Matthew 28:18-20)

You should have circled every letter except A and G.

Read Matthew 28:18-20 again and look back at the summary table on the "Disciple Phase" side. Which of these did Jesus do to the twelve disciples in Matthew 28:18-20? He released them to make disciples independently. The word *independent* does not mean that God left the scene. Jesus sent the Holy Spirit to do God's part in the process, but now the disciples were able to do their part in the process. And we are disciples today because it worked.

Paul On the Disciple Phase

Though we do not have as complete a record about Paul's discipling as we do about Jesus', we know that the apostle Paul made disciples. We can safely assume that he patterned his disciple-making after Jesus. The following table summarizes how we believe Paul discipled Timothy through the SCMD process.

Passage	SCMD	Explanation
Acts 14:20-23	Share	We believe that Paul shared the gospel — or left other disciples who shared — with Timothy.
Acts 16:1-5	Connect	We know that Paul connected with Timothy when he asked him to join his group.
Acts 17:13-14	Minister	Timothy stayed in Berea to continue discipling when Paul was forced to leave.
Acts 18:1-5		In Corinth, Timothy worked to support Paul so he could preach full-time.

From a Roman prison, Paul wrote words to Timothy that had a similar message to what Jesus told the Twelve in Matthew 28:18-20. He released Timothy to teach people who in turn could teach others as well. Sounds like disciple-making, doesn't it?

Be strong in the grace that is in Christ Jesus. And the things you have heard me say in the presence of many witnesses entrust to reliable men who will also be qualified to teach others.

(2 Timothy 2:1-2)

4. Read 2 Timothy 2:1-2 in the margin. Rewrite this verse as a personal command to you—a command given to you by Christ Himself. What might Jesus add to these words to personalize them for you specifically?

_____

_____

_____

_____

Beginning next week, we will take a closer look at each phase of the SCMD process. For now, try to master the idea of how this process intentionally uses the stages of spiritual growth to make disciples.

Review

- The disciple phase of SCMD matches up with the spiritual parent stage of disciple growth.
- In the disciple phase, leaders are released to make disciples independent of the disciple-maker being right there.

share: being intentional with the spiritually dead and spiritual infants

Intentional discipleship requires the disciple-maker to respond to a person's stage of spiritual growth. To help disciple-makers do this effectively, we have coordinated each part of the SCMD process with the corresponding stage of spiritual growth. The next four weeks we will be focusing on what to do at each stage of a person's spiritual growth and on how to utilize the SCMD process.

Even though we have assigned specific stages of growth to specific parts of the process, this process is not like an assembly line. For example, although we have associated **share** to those who are spiritually dead or in spiritual infancy, disciple-makers may still share life or new habits with someone who is a spiritual child or young adult. In general, we have found that linking the stages of growth to the SCMD process makes spiritual growth less confusing and more deliberate. A clear process helps people be more intentional at disciple-making.

Take a moment to review the **share** quadrant of the discipleship wheel.

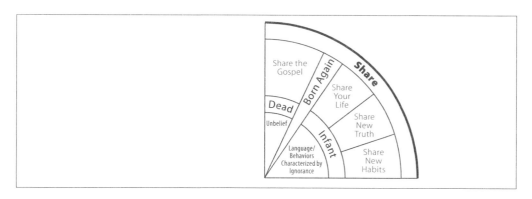

SHARING YOUR TESTIMONY

1. Read 1 Corinthians 3:6-7 in the margin. Who or what did the apostle Paul say was the cause of all spiritual growth?

God

Your answer should reflect that disciples grow because God is at work. They grow in spite of the disciple-maker's mistakes and shortcomings. The process of **share**, **connect**, **minister**, and **disciple** (SCMD) is a way for us to intentionally cooperate with God. It is a road map that can be handed off for others to follow, but without God it produces nothing. This week we will look more closely at the first step: sharing.

day 1

I planted the seed, Apollos watered it, but God made it grow. So neither he who plants nor he who waters is anything, but only God, who makes things grow.

(1 Corinthians 3:6-7)

Not Trying to Make a Sale

"The typical churched believer will die without leading a single person to a life-saving relationship with Jesus Christ." Do you remember this fact from week 1? Disciple-making begins with sharing the gospel.

Religious groups of all kinds roam through neighborhoods, searching for converts. Their missionaries knock on doors, eager to tell us that we are lost and that we need their particular beliefs to find God. How do you feel when you open the door to one of these missionaries? Do you feel excited and eager to hear what they have to say? The first few minutes of conversation set the tone. These missionaries work hard to steer the conversation toward a question or concern that leaves the person feeling helpless and in need of their teaching.

2. If you have ever had a "missionary" at your door, how did you feel? Check the appropriate boxes.

☐ Irritated
☐ Cared for
☐ Frustrated
☐ Talked at, not talked to
☐ Supported and understood
☐ Suspicious

Many people report feeling frustrated or even attacked. The word *share* communicates relationship. *Sharing* implies give and take. It also means that the person we are talking with has a choice. The disciple-maker respects a person's ability to "take it or leave it." Unlike the person who comes to the door ready to argue and debate, we listen and discuss. We do not come to "make the sale," "close the deal," or "force a decision." We trust that God is playing His role, drawing people toward a relationship with Him.

Recognizing the Spiritually Dead

In week 3, we studied the characteristics of a spiritually dead person.

3. See if you can answer these questions without looking back. Circle True (T) or False (F) below.

T F People who are spiritually dead are in the third stage of spiritual growth.
T F People who are spiritually dead often make statements like "I don't believe in God" or "There are many ways to God."
T F People who are spiritually dead need a family to connect with on their discipleship journey.
T F People who are spiritually dead are sometimes characterized by rebellion.
T F People who are spiritually dead need a place to begin to minister to others.
T F People who are spiritually dead can make disciples.

Answer key: F, T, F, T, F, F

The Importance of Being in Relationship

The old saying remains true: "They won't care about how much you know until they know how much you care."

4. Check the following perspectives toward the spiritually dead that reflect this saying:

   ☐ Every person is unique.
   ☐ When we are in a relationship with someone who is spiritually dead, we are better able to answer their questions about God.
   ☐ God gives us understanding and compassion, but at the same time we must listen to the person's story.

You should have checked all of the above. As intentional leaders (disciple-makers), we **share** our lives with unbelievers. It is far more effective to share with people our lives intersect with than it is to roam through neighborhoods, randomly knocking on doors. Whenever we meet someone who does not know Jesus, we know that he or she is spiritually dead. What would Jesus do with that person? He would offer a relationship that would lead him or her toward hearing the gospel.

Answering Questions

5. What do you think are the top three questions unbelievers struggle to understand?

   Question #1

   Who cares?

   Question #2

   Prob of evil

   Question #3

   Is sin that important?

6. How would you answer each of the questions?

   Answer #1

   Answer #2

   Answer #3

In your small group this week, discuss your questions and answers.

Preparing Your Testimony

While people may disagree about your beliefs, they cannot disagree with what God has done in your life. Your testimony is the most effective way you can share the gospel message with an unbeliever. If you have never developed your personal testimony, here is an outline that will help you do so now.

7. Write a significant event that falls under each part of this outline.

    I.   My Life Before Christ

                    ignorant

    II.   How I Accepted Christ

                    dad

    III. My Life with Christ

                    relationship

Share your testimony this week with your group.

Review

- Building a relationship paves the way for sharing the gospel with the spiritually dead.
- The two primary ways a disciple-maker shares with the spiritually dead are by answering their questions regarding faith and God and by sharing our testimonies.

Resources for Answering People's Questions

Answers to Tough Questions Skeptics Ask About the Christian Faith, by Josh McDowell and Don Stewart

The Bible Answer Book, by Hank Hanegraaff

The Case for Christ, by Lee Strobel

Know Why You Believe, by Paul E. Little

SHARING THE GOSPEL MESSAGE

day 2

Read 1 Peter 3:15 in the margin. Peter's words are at the heart of sharing with unbelievers. In this verse, he gives three directives: First, we are to make Christ our Lord. Sharing the gospel is obeying Christ. Second, we are to be prepared for every opportunity to share. We should be ready at all times to share our testimonies. Finally, Peter tells us to be gentle and respectful when we share.

There are many resources available for sharing the gospel. The following is one way that we coach people to share with unbelievers.

In your hearts set apart Christ as Lord. Always be prepared to give an answer to everyone who asks you to give the reason for the hope that you have. But do this with gentleness and respect.

(1 Peter 3:15)

Prepared to Give an Answer

First, be aware of what is happening around you:

- If you hear a "phrase from the stage," a little bell should go off.
- Remember, God has you with this person for a reason. There are things going on behind the scenes leading up to this conversation.
- Respectfully ask, "Would you like to hear what I believe about that?"

We encourage disciples to use what we refer to as the Bridge Illustration, which we have explained and illustrated below. It is simple enough to draw on a napkin over coffee and profound enough to convey the gospel clearly. The first two drawings answer an important question: "What am I being saved from?" The last drawing answers an important question: "How can I be saved?"

What Am I Being Saved From?
Step 1. God's Perfect World

God created a perfect world. His design was for us to be in relationship with Him. Because He is our creator, this relationship is the source of life.

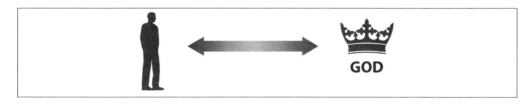

It was a perfect world. God and man walked together with no sickness, brokenness, or death.

Scriptures to reference: Genesis 1:1,26; John 6:40; 10:10. Read these Scripture passages from your Bible if the person you are sharing with is comfortable with that.

Step 2. A Broken Relationship

God did not make us robots to automatically love and obey Him. He gave us a will and freedom to choose. We chose to be our own authority. We still make this choice today. We disobey God and go our own willful way.

Scriptures to reference: Genesis 3:8-9; Isaiah 53:6; 59:2; Romans 3:23.
Read these Scripture passages from your Bible.

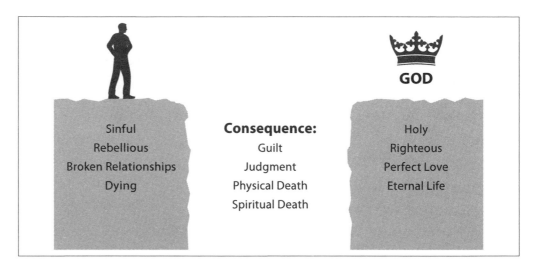

This results in separation from God, His character, and the life He gives. Separation from God comes with consequences: guilt, judgment, and death.

Scriptures to reference: Romans 6:23; Ezekiel 18:4. Read these Scriptures out loud from your Bible.

How Can I Be Saved?
Step 3. God's Remedy: Jesus Christ

On our own, there's no way we can attain the perfection and holiness required to bridge the gap between God and us. Through the ages, individuals have tried many ways without success. Good works won't do it, or religion or money or morality or philosophy (see Proverbs 14:12).

God loved us so much that He sent His Son Jesus to save us (see John 3:16). Jesus Christ is the only answer to this problem. He died on the cross and rose from the grave, paying the penalty for our sin and bridging the gap between God and people.

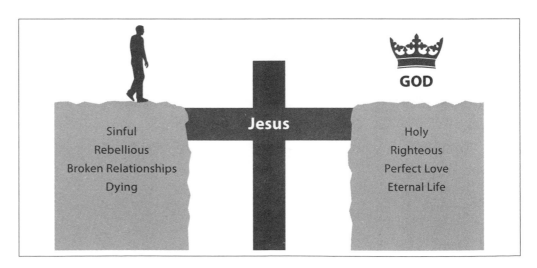

Scriptures to reference: Acts 4:12; 1 Peter 3:18; Romans 5:8; 1 Corinthians 15:3-4. Read these Scriptures from your Bible.

Step 4. Our Response

Walk through the following list, asking for a response to each question. If the person is unsure, find out what questions he or she may have.

- Is there any reason why you shouldn't cross over to God's side and be certain of eternal life? You can choose Him right now.
  - Admit that your sin has separated you from God (see Psalm 32:5; 38:18).
- Have you sinned against God and others?
  - A person is made right with God by believing in Jesus (see John 5:24; Romans 3:23-24).
- Do you believe that Jesus, the Son of God, died in your place, was buried, and rose from the dead three days later?
  - A person who believes confesses Jesus as their Lord (see Romans 10:9-10; Matthew 10:32).
- Do you confess that Jesus is God's Son and He is your Lord and Savior?
  - A person who believes repents of their sin and is baptized (see Acts 2:38).
- Are you willing to turn away from your sin and look to God for direction following the New Testament example of baptism?
  - A person who believes is being changed by Jesus (see Romans 12:1-2; James 2:14).
- Will you commit to follow Jesus, learn His Word, and join with other believers to grow to be more and more like Him?
  - Through prayer, invite Jesus Christ to come in and control your life through the Holy Spirit. (Receive Him as Lord and Savior of your life.)

A disciple-maker must be prepared to share the gospel so that those who are spiritually dead can be reborn as children of God. This is one tool that can be used to communicate the gospel and help people choose.

Review

- We have provided a tool for sharing the gospel with a spiritually dead person.
- A disciple-maker must be prepared to share the gospel so those who are spiritually dead can be reborn as children of God.

day 3

SHARING YOUR LIFE

One leader astutely observed, "Spiritual infants don't know what they don't know. How are they gonna know if you don't tell them?" Some spiritual infants may have had church exposure; others may have no idea.

When a spiritually dead person receives Christ, he or she becomes an infant. Infancy can be a demanding stage of life! Helping a spiritual infant get established requires patience and effort. Yet from the beginning we want to nudge infants toward a personal walk with Christ, one that is independent of our constant care. Today, we'll look at how disciple-makers can nurture spiritual infants so that they grow and develop into spiritual children.

Share Your Time

For spiritual infants to be healthy and to grow naturally into childhood, they need someone to take time to care for them. We can't do this effectively in a once-a-week group meeting. We need to share our lives with those we are discipling, which includes things like eating meals together, having fun together, and just hanging out with each other. It's also important for disciple-makers to be available to answer questions and respond to teachable moments.

Even though Jesus had thousands of people wanting His time, He consistently withdrew from the crowds to spend focused time with the Twelve. As disciple-makers, we must do the same.

Open Your Life to Them

1. To see how Jesus opened His life to His disciples, read the following accounts and fill in the table.

Account	Who was there?	What did Jesus do with them?
Luke 5:27-32		
Luke 7:36-50		
Luke 11:38-42		

Suggested answers are in the following chart.

Account	Who was there?	What did Jesus do with them?
Luke 5:27-32	Levi, his friends (tax gatherers and sinners), the Pharisees and Scribes	Shared a meal with them
Luke 7:36-50	Simon, the Pharisees, his friends, and a sinful woman	Shared a meal, allowed His feet to be washed, and told a story
Luke 11:38-42	The Pharisees and probably Jesus' disciples	Knew the man's heart and clarified for him what He knew to be clean versus unclean

Continue to Share Answers

2. What are the three words we used to describe the characteristics of a spiritual infant? (Look back to day 2 of week 3 for the answers if you need them.)

- ignorant
- confusion
- dependence

Life cannot stop every time a spiritual infant has questions, yet some questions cannot be put off until next week. The following exercise contains possible questions and situations that you might encounter when discipling a spiritual infant. Let's see how well you do at discerning their urgency and at addressing the question or situation.

3. An infant disciple comes to you with the following questions. Rate them on a scale of urgency.

1 means very urgent and must be answered ASAP.
2 means that we should get back to the individual if we have time.
3 means it can wait until our next regular meeting.

_____ A. "What kind of Bible should I buy?"
_____ B. "My husband and I just had an argument over my church involvement. How should I have responded?"
_____ C. "A guy at work said that Jesus will return next September. Is that true?"
_____ D. "My old pal just called and asked me to come to a party tonight. There will be drugs and alcohol there, but I think God is calling me to go be a witness. What should I do?"
_____ E. "I just read where Jesus said disciples must hate their families. Is that true?"
_____ F. "My business partner gave me reasons why he is going to leave his wife. How should I help him?"
_____ G. "How should I dress for church this Sunday?"

Answers may vary, but we think the most urgent questions are B, D, and F.

How well would you be able to answer the above questions? The idea of answering questions like this might seem a bit overwhelming, and you might be worried if you don't immediately know how to respond. One leader said that she was afraid to appear as if she didn't have all the answers. She thought her disciple would lose confidence in her.

If that's the case for you, know that it's perfectly fine if you don't have all the answers. What is important is that your faith is secure and your walk with Christ solid. When we are aware of our weaknesses, we will be more dependent on God. When a disciple sees our dependence upon Jesus, it speaks volumes. So if you get into a situation where you don't know how to respond, just say you will find the answer and get back to your disciple.

Throughout this training manual, we have given you tools and challenges not only to make disciples but also to be a disciple. A disciple-maker continues to learn and grow in his or her walk as well. Spiritual infants benefit from seeing that growth-work in you.

4. Where do you want to improve in your walk with Christ?

   ☐ Bible study
   ☐ Prayer
   ☐ Relationships with other believers
   ☐ Sharing Christ with others
   ☐ Fruit of the Spirit
   ☐ Battling temptation
   ☐ Other _____

5. Pick one area and write two things you could do to improve in these areas. Share it with your group this week.

   • _____
     _____
   • _____
     _____

Review
- Spiritual infants need us to share our lives with them, which requires time spent with them.
- Sharing life means being available to answer questions and clarify confusion.
- In the early stages, we accept a spiritual infant's dependence, all the while moving him or her to greater dependence on Jesus.

SHARING NEW TRUTH

day 4

Sharing with a spiritual infant can be demanding, which is one reason why a small group is important for the success of the discipleship process. It is critical that an infant continues to have one-on-one access to a spiritual parent even as these connections to the group grow. Though infants require personal attention, the sooner we can help them build relationships with maturing Christians, the sooner others can support the disciple-maker's nurture of the spiritual infant. These connections will also help infants grow and develop into children.

1. Based on your own commonsense knowledge of physical infants, explain why this one-on-one care cannot be neglected.

no other way to grow

Be prepared to share your answers with the group.

Let's quickly review the characteristics of spiritual infants. They are ignorant about spiritual things. They don't know what they don't know. Perhaps they have never been taught the Bible or they were taught false doctrine. It's also normal for them to be confused. As new Christians, their worldview is changing. This shift brings an unfamiliar perspective that can be uncomfortable at times. They are also marked by dependency. It is only natural for someone who is navigating unknown territory to be dependent on a guide or for a baby to depend upon parents.

Feeding Them Spiritual Milk

As we saw in week 3, new disciples need milk to grow. Milk is defined in Hebrews 5:12 as an elementary principle of the Christian life. We can begin by teaching spiritual children the basics. Acts 2:42 gives four categories of things that young Christians need to know:

- **The apostles' teaching.** This is Scripture from both the Old and New Testaments of the Bible.
- **Breaking of bread (or the Lord's Supper).** Not just Communion, but the meaning behind it, which directs us to the basics of the gospel (see 1 Corinthians 11:26; 15:3-4).
- **Prayer.** Talking with God in relationship is prayer.
- **Fellowship.** This happens in church and in large- and small-group gatherings when Christians gather to encourage each other in their faith.

2. Write two questions for each category that could help you assess where a spiritual infant is in his or her understanding of the basics.

The Bible (Example: What is the Old Testament?)

1. _How many books?_

2. _____

The gospel (Example: Did Jesus have to raise physically from the dead?)

1. _____

2. _____

Prayer (Example: Where do you go to pray?)

1. _sentence / intercessory_

2. _____

Church (Example: Do I have to go to church every week?)

1. _____

2. _____

Be prepared to share your answers with the group this week.

Keep in mind that the rest of this section is a brief overview. Volumes have been written on these subjects. Refer to the resource list at the end of this day's lesson for more help.

The Bible

Spiritual infants need to be given a broad overview of the story of the Bible from Genesis to Revelation. They need to be taught the theme of God's redemptive plan from the fall of Adam and Eve to the coming of Jesus the Savior. This does not mean they must start reading at Genesis 1:1 and finish at Revelation 22:21! We tell disciple-makers to use high points from important Old Testament stories to teach baby Christians God's story and then to slow down the story through the life of Christ.

3.   Here are ten stories from the Old Testament and ten from the New Testament. These stories are important in helping people understand God's story. They all shed light on questions that a spiritual infant might ask, such as: How did the world begin? Why is there so much trouble in the world? How have people responded to God's leading in history? Beside each story, rate how well you know it by placing a check in the appropriate column.

IMPORTANT STORIES FROM THE OLD TESTAMENT			
Story	Well	Sort of	Not at all
Creation—Genesis 1–2			
The Fall—Genesis 3			
Noah's Ark—Genesis 6–9			
Abraham's Promise—Genesis 12			
Slavery in Egypt—Exodus 1–4			
Ten Commandments—Exodus 20; Deuteronomy 5			
Israel Asks for a King—1 Samuel 8			
King David Is Chosen—1 Samuel 16			
Exile to Babylon—Daniel 1–3			
Return of Nehemiah—Nehemiah 1			

IMPORTANT STORIES FROM THE LIFE OF JESUS			
Story	Well	Sort of	Not at all
Birth—Luke 1–2			
Baptism—Matthew 3–4			
Sermon on the Mount—Matthew 5–7			
Healing of the Lame Man—Luke 5:12-26			
Feeding the Five Thousand—John 6			
Raising of Lazarus—John 11			
Crucifixion—Matthew 26–27			
Resurrection—John 20			
Jesus Commissions His Disciples—Matthew 28:18-20			
Jesus Ascends to Heaven—Acts 1			

4. Are there other stories that you think would be important? Write your additions below.

Temptation of Jesus

5. Discuss with your group this week how you think telling these stories would help a spiritual infant grow as a disciple.

The Gospel

The gospel message is found in the life of Jesus. Understanding why Jesus came and what He accomplished on the cross builds a foundation for spiritual infants. Infants often get confused about the assurance of their salvation; baby Christians often struggle with temptation. Understanding the gospel will help infants work through these issues. Many studies teach these core doctrines, including the 2:7 Series by The Navigators.

Prayer

This will be covered more in depth tomorrow, so let's move on to new truth about the church.

The Church

Spiritual infants may carry distaste for organized religion into their new life as a disciple. The church is referred to in Scripture as the body of Christ (see Romans 12:4-5), the bride of Christ (see Revelation 19:7-9), and the temple of God (see 1 Corinthians 3:16-17). The early church placed high priority upon gathering in fellowship. We need to share these truths with infants.

Many things that we do in church or even in small groups may confuse spiritual infants. They might ask, "Why do we sing?" "Why do we go every week?" "What is the offering for?" Infants can all too easily go through the ritual without understanding the meaning. This puts them on a fast track to being religious instead of in relationship with God.

6. Are there any areas of biblical truth that you are ignorant or confused about? If so, write your questions here. Take time this week to find the answers.

Review

- When sharing new truth, the disciple-maker begins by listening in order to assess how much a person already knows.
- Young disciples frequently have common questions that a disciple-maker can be prepared to answer.

- Sharing new truth with spiritual infants includes teaching the foundations of the Bible, the church, the gospel, and prayer.

Resources for Understanding the Bible

30 Days to Understanding the Bible in 15 Minutes a Day, by Max Anders

Talk thru the Bible, by Bruce Wilkinson and Kenneth Boa

day 5

SHARING NEW HABITS

In week 3, we noted the habits spiritual infants need to establish. Individual personality influences these choices, yet all disciples need a few core habits. Today we look at how to help them develop these habits (or disciplines).

The Habit of Bible Reading

Though it takes physical babies a long time to learn to feed themselves, spiritual infants can immediately begin to develop this habit. As spiritual infants grow in their understanding of the Bible, they will find it less confusing to read it on their own. Here are some tips to help them get started with their Bibles. Choose two that you think would be most helpful:

- Help them choose a version of the Bible that is easy to understand.
- Hold them accountable to a regular time of Bible reading, starting with a goal of three times per week.
- Have them choose a specific location where they will do their Bible reading.
- Help them develop a Bible-reading plan. Start slowly. We often recommend that people start with the book of Mark, as it focuses on Jesus and is not too long.

Share this habit by making your personal Bible reading a regular part of your discussions. Don't assume that the spiritual infant knows what to do.[4] As a new Christian matures, Bible reading will give way to more in-depth study and you can begin to introduce tools and methods for Bible study. But start with encouraging the disciple to have regular times of Bible reading.

Disciple-makers can also help spiritual infants develop activities that will reinforce what they read, such as journaling about what they learn, writing out prayers, highlighting things that are meaningful or important in their Bibles, and keeping track of their Bible reading with a reading log. All of these are good ways to reinforce this habit.

1. Write out a six-session Bible-reading plan that you think a spiritual infant could easily master.

Example:

Day	Scripture	Activity
Day 1	Mark 1–2	When you're done reading, write a one-paragraph summary of each chapter in your own words.
Day 2	Mark 3–4	Pick one thing Jesus did or taught that you think applies directly to you and highlight it in your Bible.

Day	Scripture	Activity
1		
2		
3		
4		
5		
6		

The Habit of Sharing the Gospel

Most spiritual infants have no problem finding someone to share the gospel with because many of their friends are not believers. Infants can share by simply telling others how they came to Christ, or they can present the gospel using a few verses highlighted in their Bible. The diagrams we covered in day 2 of this week are easy to remember and pencil out on a napkin.

2. Draw the diagrams from memory here. Then go back and see if you remembered them accurately.

Diagram 1

Diagram 2

Diagram 3

The best way to share this habit with a spiritual infant is to model it. If you don't share the gospel with others, telling a baby Christian to do so will not work. You can also give new Christians a chance to practice sharing the gospel. For instance, have the disciple practice drawing the diagrams on a napkin as he or she might when visiting someone in a coffee shop. Listen as your disciple becomes fluent in sharing his or her testimony. Help your disciple select a few key verses to highlight in his or her Bible.

Also, encourage your disciple to identify a list of people to pray for who need to know Jesus. Pray together that these people might come to know Christ and for opportunities to share Christ. Celebrate what God does, and rejoice with your disciple when he or she gets to be a part of seeing someone come to faith. These actions will help a spiritual infant develop the habit of sharing the gospel.

God so loved the world that he gave his one and only Son, that whoever believes in him shall not perish but have eternal life.
(John 3:16)

Salvation is found in no one else, for there is no other name under heaven given to men by which we must be saved.
(Acts 4:12)

If you confess with your mouth, "Jesus is Lord," and believe in your heart that God raised him from the dead, you will be saved. For it is with your heart that you believe and are justified, and it is with your mouth that you confess and are saved.
(Romans 10:9-10)

3. The following verses are good for sharing the gospel. Read them in the margin and then write one or two sentences that a person could use to explain each verse.

John 3:16	
Acts 4:12	Only one way
Romans 10:9-10	

Be prepared to discuss your sentences in your group this week.

4. What other verses would you use?

_____

_____

_____

_____

The Habit of Praying

Spiritual infants need to *learn* to pray. Teaching about prayer is not as important as practicing prayer. In other words, infants can learn a lot simply by praying with you. Pushing through the roadblock of being self-conscious will eliminate a fear that can cripple the spiritual growth of a disciple. Forming this habit while the cement of spiritual growth is wet will pay dividends for the disciple throughout life.

5. Match the following aspects of prayer with the correct description.

C Adoration	A. Admitting my shortcomings and failures to God and trusting in His forgiveness
A Confession	B. Asking God to help others who are hurting and in need
B Requests	C. Praising God for His awesome and holy character

Answer key: C, A, and B

The Habit of Church Attendance

New Christians must develop the habit of regular attendance in church and small group. Sunday morning may have been a time to sleep in, play golf, or do yard work. Citing a verse from the Bible may not be enough to convince some. They need to know why this habit is important.

6. Read Hebrews 10:24-25 in the margin. What two reasons does the writer of Hebrews give for regular church attendance?

- _____
  _____

- _____
  _____

Let us consider how we may spur one another on toward love and good deeds. Let us not give up meeting together, as some are in the habit of doing, but let us encourage one another—and all the more as you see the Day approaching.

(Hebrews 10:24-25)

First, regular church attendance gives believers the opportunity to know (consider) each other in order to promote (spur) love and good deeds. Second, church serves as a refueling station where we can be encouraged.

When spiritual infants attend church, they are bound to have other questions. Each question presents an opportunity for discipleship.

7. Match the question from day 4 of this week with the habit it leads to for a new Christian.

C Why do we sing?	A. The habit of fellowship
A Why go every week?	B. The habit of tithing
B What is the offering for?	C. The habit of worship

Answer key: C, A, and B

Evaluating Their Growth

Don't set a time limit on how long a disciple will be a spiritual infant. Instead, pay attention to his or her characteristics. For example:

- John has developed a fairly consistent habit of reading his Bible. He is learning how to feed himself spiritually.
- He comes to church each week and has good questions when he meets for discipleship.
- He is becoming more comfortable with praying in the group.

All of these are characteristics that show that John is moving into the childhood stage of discipleship.

8. Write a brief prayer that you, as a spiritual parent, might pray for someone who is a spiritual infant.

_____

_____

_____

_____

Review

- New habits form a foundation for the future.
- Disciple-makers need to intentionally help spiritual infants develop the habits of Bible reading, sharing the gospel, prayer, and church participation.

connect: helping spiritual children grow

Today we will return to a theme that we have explored repeatedly in the past eight weeks—relationships. As the vehicles that God designed for the discipleship journey, relationships are necessary at every stage of the disciple's growth.

RELATIONSHIPS MATTER

Brandon Guindon and Jim Putman once attended a conference designed to help pastors and church leaders reach out to non-Christians in other countries. In a small-group breakout session, the group spent some time getting to know each other. Brandon and Jim shared about hunting together, their friendship, and what God was doing in our church. It was a fun time, and the group bonded immediately.

The discussion went deeper as the group talked about struggles and fears and about being transparent as leaders. God was working in a powerful way. Soon Doug, their facilitator, was in tears. Like a car skidding to a stop, the group halted. Jim put a hand on Doug's knee and asked, "What's going on with you?"

Through his tears, Doug said, "I have no friends. No one knows me. This group is more transparent than I have ever been with anyone in my life. I feel closer to you guys than to my own staff, and I just met you."

Doug was the pastor of a large church, but he had no connection with anyone and felt separated from others and God. He felt that if he were to be transparent and share his struggles with those in his church, he would be ridiculed and probably let go.

How in the world did Doug come to that conclusion? God designed His church to be connected in deep abiding relationships, but Doug was alone and hurting. As a leader, he was hindered from effectively make disciples because discipleship requires relationships, and relationships require transparency. Do you know anyone like Doug?

How About You?

1. Check the quote that most accurately describes you:

   ☑ I can make it on my own without telling others what is going on with me.
   ☐ I don't like to be transparent, but if I have to I will.
   ☐ I believe that connection to other believers is essential to my spiritual growth.
   ☐ I can list three people right now that help me in my spiritual growth.

   Are you more like Doug or more like the person reflected in the last statement above?

We encourage you to be more intentional in your connections with people, especially those you disciple. Remember, a disciple-maker must be connected to God and others (see Luke 10:27).

Connection Means Investment

Take a moment to review the **connect** quadrant of the discipleship wheel.

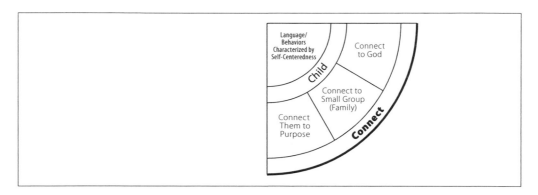

2. What are the three essential connections that a disciple-maker should help a spiritual child make?

- _____
- _____
- _____

In the rest of this lesson, we are going to focus on how disciple-makers build relationships with spiritual children that help them connect in those three ways.

3. Check the ways you might build a connecting relationship with disciples who are spiritual children:

☐ Taking time in your schedule to get to know them
☐ Listening to their story
☐ Sharing personal stories so they can relate to you
☐ Checking up on their well-being
☐ Holding them accountable for applying what they are learning about being a Christian
☐ Empathizing as they experience "growing pains"

We hope you checked all of the ways listed. Here is a summary of those answers:

- As intentional leaders, we need to carve out room in our schedules to spend time with spiritual children. Time together needs to center around the relationship and not just tasks we might do.

- The give-and-take of listening to our disciples' histories and sharing our own stories strengthens the bond of connection.
- Intentional leaders try not to assume that others are okay but probe deeper with questions about their well-being.
- As disciples, spiritual children should be growing and maturing. The disciple-maker intentionally helps them by checking up on their progress and helping them apply the new things they are learning.
- Finally, relationships deepen when disciple-makers let spiritual children know they are not the only ones to have the struggles that come with this stage of growth. Empathizing with disciples is an important way to connect with them.

Jesus spent time in close proximity to the people He discipled. He walked, ate, prayed, talked, ministered, cried, and traveled with them. They knew He was concerned for their welfare by the way He related to them. In all likelihood, the most consistent impression they had was *Jesus loves me.*

4. Read John 13:1-5 in the margin. How did Jesus show the full extent of His love to the disciples?

Served them

_____

_____

_____

5. Place a checkmark by the commitments that you think would fit you best in building relational connection with spiritual children.

- ☐ Scheduling a time to discuss over coffee questions they have or to listen to their story
- ☐ Inviting them to my house for dinner or dessert to get to know them and their families better
- ☐ Meeting them after church for lunch at a local café
- ☐ Spending time with them doing something we both like that is not related to church

6. List ways you will be more intentionally relational with some of the spiritual children God has placed in your life.

It was just before the Passover Feast. Jesus knew that the time had come for him to leave this world and go to the Father. Having loved his own who were in the world, he now showed them the full extent of his love.

The evening meal was being served, and the devil had already prompted Judas Iscariot, son of Simon, to betray Jesus. Jesus knew that the Father had put all things under his power, and that he had come from God and was returning to God; so he got up from the meal, took off his outer clothing, and wrapped a towel around his waist. After that, he poured water into a basin and began to wash his disciples' feet, drying them with the towel that was wrapped around him.

(John 13:1-5)

Name	Ways to be more relational

7. Pray for the names you have listed.

Review

- A disciple-maker helps spiritual children connect with God, other disciples, and their purpose.
- An intentional leader connects relationally with spiritual children to help these things happen.

HELPING SPIRITUAL CHILDREN CONNECT WITH THEIR FATHER

day 2

Yesterday we looked at how disciple-makers can connect relationally with spiritual children. Today we want to examine what a connection with God looks like and how intentional leaders can help foster this vital connection.

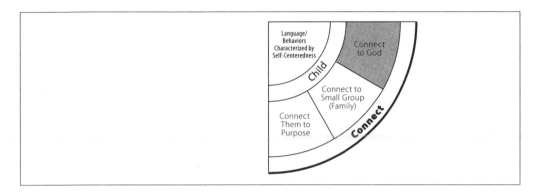

It Begins with You

Disciple-makers must be connected to God in a deep, abiding relationship. We cannot help others have a relationship with God when we do not. Our connection with God changes us. That relationship becomes the source of our ability to connect others to God as well.

1. In the chart on day 3 of week 2, you listed ways you can spend time with Jesus. Alongside each, you rated how frequently you spend time with Him in that way. Go back and review your answers.

    *   What do you feel are the strengths of your relationship with God?

    _____

    _____

    _____

    *   What areas of your relationship could be improved?

    _____

    _____

    _____

    _____

Your relationship with God is very personal. Please be balanced in your assessment. Here are a couple examples of how disciples can have a skewed perspective:

*   Linda felt she was very connected to God. She proved it by constantly telling others how strong her prayer life was. What she didn't know was that she sounded like she had spiritual pride.
*   Tom perpetually put his spiritual life down. No matter how much he read his Bible or prayed, he always thought he could do more. Instead of enjoying a

relationship with God, he felt that his connection with Him was inferior to every other Christian.

2. What are some things you do to be in relationship with God that you could show someone else how to do?

_____

_____

_____

_____

_____

Your answers might include learning to pray, reading and studying the Bible, and memorizing Scripture. Spiritual children also build their connection to God by worshipping together, attending church functions, and participating in a small group. Key habits such as these help them learn to understand God's Word and know His will. Without these habits, disciples will remain spiritual children, ignorant of God's plan and stunted in their growth.

3. Circle the letter of the statements that reflect what disciple-makers should help spiritual children learn so they can build their relationship with God.

A. God hears and answers prayers.
B. God has no plan or design for spiritual growth.
C. God can use other Christians to help us relate to God.
D. People who are connected to God have to be able to pray all night.
E. Corporate worship can help us connect with God.
F. God is removed from our daily lives.
G. The Word of God provides direction for our lives.
H. Other non-Christian religions help us connect relationally with God.

We hope you circled all but B, D, F, and H. When people you disciple learn to pray, search the Word, and become involved in the family of God, they can begin to build a personal relationship with God that is meaningful and accurate. They can grow beyond being spoon-fed all of their spiritual nutrition and start connecting with God personally.

Dependent upon God and Less upon Me

Spiritual children need to learn how to connect with God personally. Consequently, the disciple-maker should not do everything for them. It is tempting to become an answer person, like a walking spiritual dictionary, but that is not best. We do not want disciples to be solely dependent on us. Intentional leaders help spiritual children use their connection with us to draw closer in their own relationship with God. Letting them find answers on their own is good. Allowing them to struggle through different issues without providing a shortcut answer for them helps them grow in their dependence on God.

The apostle Paul discusses this issue in 1 Corinthians 3:3-4. He was concerned because the Corinthian believers were connecting primarily to a certain leader instead of to God and His family.

4. Read what Paul says in 1 Corinthians 3:6-9 in the margin. Answer the following questions:

- Who makes us grow?

  God

- How do different leaders help us grow?

  they do the right thing at the right time

- Which is most important, a disciple's connection with God or with the disciple-maker?

  w/ God

> *I planted the seed, Apollos watered it, but God made it grow. So neither he who plants nor he who waters is anything, but only God, who makes things grow. The man who plants and the man who waters have one purpose, and each will be rewarded according to his own labor. For we are God's fellow workers; you are God's field, God's building.*
> *(1 Corinthians 3:6-9)*

Paul directs people to the source of their growth: God. Disciple-makers help spiritual children grow by doing the same.

5. Where do you think you fall on the dependence scale? Place an "X" where you think you are.

I think I would be most likely to foster a disciple's dependence on . . .

Me, the disciple-maker   God and Me   God

Review

- Disciple-makers must have a solid connection to God if they are to give spiritual children help in their own personal relationships with God.
- Disciple-makers should intentionally show spiritual children how to build a relationship with God.
- Disciple-makers should avoid fostering a spiritual child's overdependence upon them.

day 3

CONNECTING SPIRITUAL CHILDREN WITH GOD'S FAMILY

The people we disciple belong to God's family, the church. They are part of a team and have a role to play in helping the church succeed in fulfilling the mission Jesus gave us. Their church family also gives them a new web of relationships. In a world of broken relationships, the family of God can help spiritual children grow as disciples.

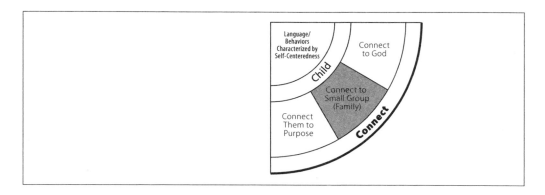

As you begin today, take a moment to reflect about your own connection to your small group. How has it changed over the past nine weeks?

A Real Life Ministries Story

Tim had recently given his life to Christ. One night he came to Brandon Guindon's small group with a frustrated look on his face and body language that showed he was tense and angry. After the group was over, Brandon asked Tim what was wrong. Tim said that he had listened to the sermon the previous Sunday and decided that he should just quit the "whole Christian thing." Shocked, Brandon asked what had happened.

The sermon, which had been about men being spiritual leaders at home, left Tim confused, embarrassed, and frustrated. He had grown up without a father and said that he had no idea how to do things such as pray with his wife or have devotions with his children. He felt overwhelmed and had no idea how to be a spiritual leader.

1. Read Hebrews 3:12-13 and 10:24-25 in the margin and write three reasons why Tim needs his connection to the small group more than ever.

- _____
- _____
- _____

Your answers might include meeting together so he could be encouraged and spurring on toward love and good deeds.

See to it, brothers, that none of you has a sinful, unbelieving heart that turns away from the living God. But encourage one another daily, as long as it is called Today, so that none of you may be hardened by sin's deceitfulness.

(Hebrews 3:12-13)

Let us consider how we may spur one another on toward love and good deeds. Let us not give up meeting together, as some are in the habit of doing, but let us encourage one another—and all the more as you see the Day approaching.

(Hebrews 10:24-25)

2. If Tim had been only a Sunday morning spectator who was not connected to a small group, what do you think would have happened to him?

Most likely, Tim would have left the church with feelings of inadequacy or even resentment toward God. This would have impacted his wife and children. Fortunately, the family of God, especially his small group, lived out their role as outlined in Hebrews and prevented such an unnecessary tragedy.

Connections Modeled

When Tim voiced his frustration, the small group played key roles. God used Brandon to challenge Tim and give him hope that together they would work through his frustrations. Another small-group member, John, gave Tim specific ideas about how to do devotions with his kids. Damon shared with Tim his own fears of praying with his wife and how God helped him through it. Together, the family of God surrounded Tim and gave him the concrete help he needed to begin new habits that enabled him to become a spiritual leader in his home. God used Tim's spiritual family to help Tim, a spiritual child, grow.

3. Think of someone in your small group or someone you know who is experiencing struggles. Write the person's initials here. _____ _____

4. How could the family of God encourage this person through this problem? (Be specific.)

----

5. Read the verses again and then, in the following diagram, look at the practical things Tim's spiritual family did for him. Circle the things you and your group could do for the struggling person you know. This week in your group time or with another person, talk about how you can help this person grow.

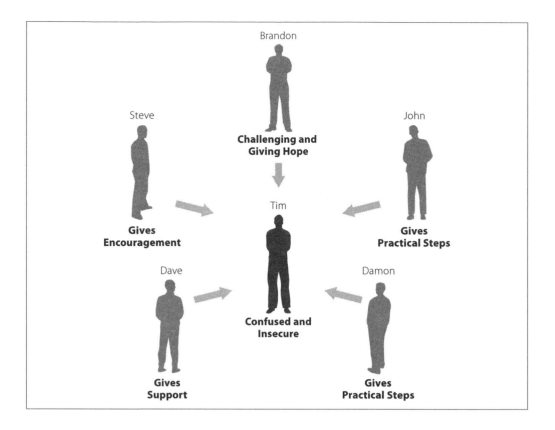

As Tim's experience illustrates, when spiritual children are connected to other believers, they receive the encouragement and help they need to grow up in their faith.

6. Reread Hebrew 3:12-13 and 10:24-25 as you pray for the friend whose initials you wrote above. Check the things here that you think you could do immediately for friends experiencing one of the negative things mentioned in these verses.

☐ Pay attention to childlike behavior
☐ Give encouragement
☐ Point him or her to biblical truth
☐ Genuinely care for the person
☐ Confront him or her and point out specific sins
☐ Hold him or her accountable
☐ Give grace and support
☐ Help the person be aware of temptations
☐ Bear with the person as he or she grows

7. What are the three connections the intentional disciple-maker helps spiritual children make?

- Connect them to _____ God _____
- Connect them to _____ B Study _____
- Connect them to _____ purpose _____

8. Write Hebrews 3:12-13 in your own words.

_____

_____

_____

_____

Be prepared to share your answers with the group.

Review

- Spiritual children need to be connected to other disciples.
- Believers can help each other by meeting together, encouraging each other, and spurring one another on to growth.
- Intentional disciple-makers connect spiritual children to others in the body of Christ as well as minister to them personally.

day 4

CONNECTING SPIRITUAL CHILDREN TO THEIR PURPOSE IN CHRIST

Healthy things grow, and when spiritual children deepen their connection to God and a church family, they naturally mature. The Holy Spirit works in their lives as they begin to understand biblical truth through their devotional times and prayer. With the help of the Holy Spirit, their church family can support them and bring clarity to biblical truth.

An intentional next step for the disciple-maker is to help spiritual children see beyond themselves—to see that they are saved for kingdom purposes.

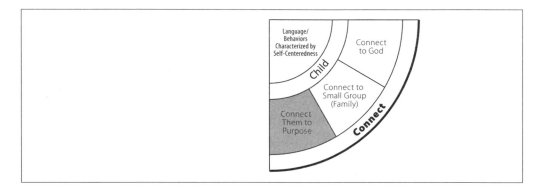

What Would You Do?

Imagine for a moment that you share an office with a young woman who is spiritually dead. You share Christ with her; she becomes a Christian and gets connected to a small group. As a spiritual parent, you continue to meet with your friend and disciple her. She is growing spiritually and developing new habits: daily devotions, a prayer life, and a commitment to attending church and her small group. Because of the time you spend together and your deepening relationship, you notice her gifts and abilities. You begin to see how God could potentially use her to impact others. As an intentional leader you are at a crossroads in the discipleship journey.

1. Check the statement that best fits how you would respond at this juncture:

    ☐ I would do nothing yet. She doesn't know the Bible well enough to serve in the church.
    ☐ I would encourage her to keep growing. Someday God is going to use her, but right now she is not ready. She might get hurt or become disappointed.
    ☐ I would challenge her, pointing out the abilities she has, and invite her to serve in some way so she could begin seeing her purpose in God's mission.

Did you check the last option? The transition to service is a critical link to becoming a spiritual young adult. Without a connection to their purpose as disciples, spiritual children can become stunted in their growth. They begin to rely on a spiritual parent or others in the church in an unhealthy way. As intentional leaders, we don't want a church full of infants and spiritual children; we want mature disciples who can disciple others.

2. Read Ephesians 4:12 in the margin. Paraphrase the following words or phrases in your own words.

Prepare God's people for works of service, so that the body of Christ may be built up.

(Ephesians 4:12)

- Prepare

  train/disciple

- Works of service

  ministry deeds   meet needs

- Built up

  so people can grow

Be prepared to share your answers in your small group.

God intends for disciple-makers to prepare God's people. This means to grow them up, to help them mature. We believe that *works of service* encompasses anything from holding babies to serving as a leader of a small group. Works of service do not earn our salvation, but they do build up the church. "Built up" means the church has grown in number and the people are growing to be more like Jesus.

A Spiritual Parent's Hesitations

Despite this need, disciple-makers are sometimes hesitant to connect spiritual children to a larger purpose. We fear that they will fail, say something wrong, misquote or misuse the Bible, or give others the wrong impression.

3. What if something like this happened with your disciple? Write a way that you could correct each of the following mistakes if they occurred. Discuss your answers in your small group.

- Disciple 1 – It has come to your attention that a person you are discipling said that the people at the church across town are probably not real Christians.

- Disciple 2 – In small group, the person you are discipling said that the phrase "The early bird catches the worm" is in the Bible somewhere.

Certainly we need a balance between moving children too quickly into service and encouraging them to serve. Keep it simple. You are helping them think about how God designed them to serve in the mission of Christ. Connecting them to God's bigger purpose is paving the way for the next stage of spiritual growth: spiritual young adulthood.

Making These Connections

All three connections are important. Intentional leaders do their part to help spiritual children connect. We pray, encourage, and wait patiently as God grows them and they respond.

4. Who helped you most in learning to develop a personal relationship with God?

_____

_____

5. Who helped you most to get connected to a group of Christians who would support you?

_____

_____

6. What helped you most to connect to God's greater purpose for your life?

_____

_____

_____

_____

Be prepared to discuss your answers with your small group.

Review

- The spiritual child needs to connect to the purpose of God's mission.
- Intentional disciple-makers should challenge even spiritually young children to get involved in simple service.

HANDLING CONFLICTS

day 5

We change the pace today to look at an unavoidable fact of life: We will face conflict in our relationships, including with those we disciple. Today we are going to present biblical ways of handling conflicts.

Conflict Is Normal

Conflict is a normal part of relationships, yet for many the word *conflict* creates anxiety. There seem to be two extremes when it comes to conflict: Some people ignore it, hoping it will go away, whereas others refuse to take any responsibility, making the conflict worse.

Most of us fall somewhere between these two extremes. As an intentional leader, you will need tools to work through conflict so that your relationships are not only preserved but also deepened. God does not allow us to hide from relationship problems. Intentional leaders must model, practice, and teach God's principles for unity to those we disciple.

A Biblical Process and Principles

Here are six steps gathered from many Bible verses that can guide you in resolving conflict between you and another person:

- Step 1: Acknowledge the conflict or offense, and go to the person involved.
- Step 2: Talk to the person in private.
- Step 3: Ask if you have offended the person. If so, confess your sin and ask forgiveness.
- Step 4: If you are the one offended, consider overlooking the offense.
- Step 5: If the person has sinned, show your brother or sister his or her fault with a humble spirit, using the Bible.
- Step 6: Restore the relationship with the kind of grace Jesus has given you.

Remember, the goal is to win over your brother or sister in Christ through a biblical process (see Matthew 18:15-19). When connecting with a spiritual child, conflict may occur. Intentional leaders must do their best to work toward reconciliation and unity. We should not expect spiritual children to do this on their own. As spiritual parents, it is our responsibility to lead people we disciple to unity and peace. Being connected relationally means that we do not drop a relationship as soon as it becomes difficult.

1. Read (in the margin) the following verses that shed light on relational difficulty and conflict. After each, write a summary sentence, highlighting helpful hints for managing conflict.

- Matthew 7:3-5   *don't judge*
  _____
  _____
  _____

Why do you look at the speck of sawdust in your brother's eye and pay no attention to the plank in your own eye? How can you say to your brother, "Let me take the speck out of your eye," when all the time there is a plank in your own eye? You hypocrite, first take the plank out of your own eye, and then you will see clearly to remove the speck from your brother's eye.
(Matthew 7:3-5)

Anyone who claims to be in the light but hates his brother is still in the darkness. Whoever loves his brother lives in the light, and there is nothing in him to make him stumble. But whoever hates his brother is in the darkness and walks around in the darkness; he does not know where he is going, because the darkness has blinded him.
(1 John 2:9-11)

Bear with each other and forgive whatever grievances you may have against one another. Forgive as the Lord forgave you. And over all these virtues put on love, which binds them all together in perfect unity.
Let the peace of Christ rule in your hearts, since as members of one body you were called to peace. And be thankful.
(Colossians 3:13-15)

As a prisoner for the Lord, then, I urge you to live a life worthy of the calling you have received. Be completely humble and gentle; be patient, bearing with one another in love. Make every effort to keep the unity of the Spirit through the bond of peace.
(Ephesians 4:1-3)

- 1 John 2:9-11

  primacy of love

- Colossians 3:13-15

  Forgive and restore

- Ephesians 4:1-3

  humility/patience

There is no simple formula for handling relational conflict, but these verses provide wisdom from God's Word that can guide us through difficulties.

2. Using the six steps above and your thoughts from these verses, write out two or three guidelines that will help you navigate through relational conflict with those you disciple.

-

-

-

Make it a priority to discuss your ideas in your small group this week.

3. What are some unresolved conflicts you have with those you are discipling?

4. What is God calling you to do to resolve the conflicts?

Review
- Conflict is inevitable in relationships.
- The disciple-maker/spiritual parent needs to help spiritual children resolve conflict.
- The Bible gives us wise counsel for dealing with conflict.

minister: helping young adults help others

Not long ago, Jim Putman was talking with a man from another church who made it clear that he viewed the church he attended as "his church." This man had been there long before the current minister, and he felt that his tenure entitled him to critique everything. "This rock-and-roll singing in service has to stop," he said. His list went on and on: kids wearing hats inside, people smelling like cigarette smoke, not being able to know everyone's name. Everything on the list seemed rooted in this man's desire for personal comfort. He made no mention of his concern for others and had no report about how he was serving in the church. Though he had been a church member for years, this man was still a spiritual child. He had never grown spiritually, and ministry to others was a foreign concept.

MAKING THE TRANSITION

day 1

Growth from spiritual childhood to spiritual young adulthood happens in the context of ministry. It is a transformational process that comes from connecting to God's greater purpose. God challenges and convicts disciples to realize that the game is much bigger than their personal comfort and preferences. It is not all about them. He shows them they are to change from being self-focused to genuinely caring about the needs of others.

1. Circle the following words that you think are synonyms for the term *ministry* as it is used in the New Testament:

Service	Assistance	Department
Avoid	Helping	Aid

The words that are not synonyms for ministry are *department* and *avoid*. Ministry can help hearts change and move a disciple from spiritual childhood to the young adult stage. As intentional leaders model service/ministry, God prompts the disciple to start looking beyond his or her own needs. However, disciples must be willing to move beyond their own comfort to value the needs of the hurting world around them.

Becoming God-and-Others-Focused

2. Following are a list of phrases from believers who are spiritual children (self-focused) and those who are spiritual young adults (others-focused). Place a "C" by the spiritual child statements and a "YA" next to spiritual young adult statements.

_____ 1. I love my small group because they take care of me.

_____ 2. My church meets my needs, and that makes me happy.

_____ 3. I am excited to see these two new couples in our group.

_____ 4. I never want my small group to change because new people make me nervous.

_____ 5. I noticed that my friend has not been in church. I need to call her and make sure she is okay.

_____ 6. There is a need in the youth ministry. Is God telling me I need to help?

So how did you do? Statements 1, 2, and 4 should be marked C. The rest should have a YA beside them.

Jesus said to his disciples, "If anyone would come after me, he must deny himself and take up his cross and follow me. For whoever wants to save his life will lose it, but whoever loses his life for me will find it."

(Matthew 16:24-25)

3. Read Matthew 16:24-25 in the margin and mark an "X" on the line to indicate where you are today on the denying-self scale.

●————————————————————————————————————●

It's all about me.   It's about whom   I see needs around   God's grace causes
                          I like and me.   me and feel for   me to respond to
                                                  them.   help others.

A true disciple learns to deny self and rely on God. Christians who are immature in the faith (spiritual children or infants) may be involved in ministry, but their hearts are not God-centered or others-focused. Unfortunately, people sometimes do ministry for selfish reasons.

Jesus called them together and said, "You know that the rulers of the Gentiles lord it over them, and their high officials exercise authority over them. Not so with you. Instead, whoever wants to become great among you must be your servant, and whoever wants to be first must be your slave—just as the Son of Man did not come to be served, but to serve, and to give his life as a ransom for many."

(Matthew 20:25-28)

4. Read Matthew 20:25-28 in the margin. When Jesus said, "Not so with you," what was He emphasizing?

_____

_____

_____

Jesus meant that service is the mark of a disciple. There was no Plan B.

5. Write in your own words God's Plan A for a disciple to achieve greatness.

_____

_____

_____

6. Why do you think there was no Plan B?

_____

_____

_____

_____

Jesus embodied God's Plan A of servanthood, and we are to follow His example. Service is not an option. It is God's heart and Jesus' example.

7. Check three behaviors you could model to help a disciple understand a servant's heart.

☐ Giving credit to God for good things
☐ Taking the credit for success
☐ Being in charge
☐ Loving the difficult person
☐ Helping others joyfully
☐ Avoiding difficult people

The correct answers should be obvious: giving credit to God, loving difficult people, and helping others.

How can you tell when those you are discipling are having a heart change? Like Jesus, you intentionally listen to their words and observe their actions. Look for the shift that God brings about as they show genuine concern for the needs of others and become less focused on their own comfort, preferences, and recognition. When this happens, you know they are ready to move into the ministry phase.

8. What are some service or church ministry opportunities you have access to currently that could be used to help disciples grow?

Review

- A spiritual child has made the transition into young adulthood when there is evidence that his or her heart has changed from being self-centered to being God-centered and others-focused.
- The disciple-maker intentionally looks for these changes as a cue that the disciple is ready for ministry/service.

day 2

EQUIPPING TO MINISTER

The intentional leader trains disciples to serve and to develop the attitudes and behaviors of a spiritual young adult. We call this equipping for ministry.

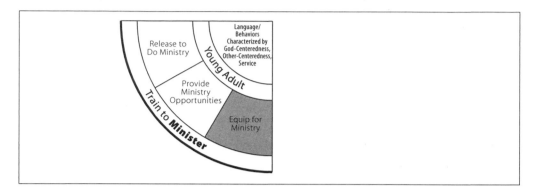

Churches often rely on Bible colleges or seminaries to equip people for ministry, yet all Christians are called to ministry, regardless of their formal education (see 1 Peter 4:10-11). If we limit ministry to those who have formal training, we force a majority of the church body to live in the spiritual nursery. God-centered service is the key difference between spiritual children and spiritual young adults.

1. Using the diagram above, what are the three things an intentional disciple-maker does to train a spiritual young adult?

   - _____
     _____
   - _____
     _____
   - _____
     _____

Tasks or People?

Equipping disciples to minister is more than giving them a task to accomplish in the church. Some tasks—such as handing out bulletins, ushering people to their seats, or singing on a worship team—are important for running the Sunday morning service, but they do not train disciples to minister relationally. Disciple-makers need to intentionally guide spiritual young adults through the relational dynamics of ministry as well as give them ministry tasks.

2. Where do you fall on the line of what's important? Place an "X" where you fall.

A job completed
on time

Everybody getting
along in harmony

Knowing that you did what needed to be done	Knowing that people were helped

Being sure a task is completed	Making sure people grow spiritually in the process

Marking toward the left on the lines above indicates that you are more task-oriented. The more you marked to the right, the more people-related you are. Both tasks and people are important, but tasks are not more important than people. Tasks are discipling opportunities. Young adults often serve with unrealistic expectations of themselves and others. That's why equipping them for ministry involves preparing them for disappointment and for success.

Preparing Disciples for Disappointment

3. The following are potential pitfalls a disciple might fall into while serving in ministry. Check the ones you have experienced.

- ☐ Feeling like a failure because nobody noticed
- ☐ Losing motivation because no one said thanks
- ☐ Being hurt because someone was critical
- ☐ Wanting to quit because my efforts didn't measure up to what others had done
- ☐ Being surprised when people had different expectations of me

4. Jesus prepared His disciples for extreme rejection. Read Matthew 5:11-12 in the margin. What motivation did Jesus tell them to have so they wouldn't give up?

_____

_____

_____

_____

Blessed are you when people insult you, persecute you and falsely say all kinds of evil against you because of me. Rejoice and be glad, because great is your reward in heaven, for in the same way they persecuted the prophets who were before you.

(Matthew 5:11-12)

Spiritual young adults need to find their security in their connection with God. Even though no one else may notice, God sees what they are doing out of their love for Him and for others. When no one says thank you or even criticizes us, Jesus said that God gives heavenly rewards. When disciples understand this, they are less likely to be discouraged. As intentional leaders, we need to teach these truths proactively. This will help young adults deal with disappointments when they come. It is an important part of their connection to God.

Preparing Disciples for Successes

There is nothing like success in ministry. The exhilaration of a job well done can be intoxicating; however, disciples who are new to serving can overestimate their abilities.

5. Read the following scenarios and identify ways the disciple could have overestimated himself or herself or the situation.

- Michael learned to play a worship song on the guitar and sing it without looking at the words. When the small-group leader invited him to sing his song, everyone joined in and sang the chorus with him. The next week, Michael announced to his leader that he had volunteered to be the new worship leader for the youth ministry.

What kind of potential problems might Michael have set himself up for?

_____

_____

_____

- Susan just returned from a prayer retreat and is excited about her new commitment to prayer. She already planned a weekend and reserved lodging for her small group so she could teach the group how to pray.

What things has Susan potentially misjudged that may set her up for problems?

_____

_____

_____

The seventy-two returned with joy and said, "Lord, even the demons submit to us in your name."

He replied, "I saw Satan fall like lightning from heaven. I have given you authority to trample on snakes and scorpions and to overcome all the power of the enemy; nothing will harm you. However, do not rejoice that the spirits submit to you, but rejoice that your names are written in heaven."

(Luke 10:17-20)

If you were discipling Michael, you would need to be careful not to squelch his enthusiasm; however, you would also need to help him understand the potential challenges of being a worship leader. Leading worship is demanding, both musically and spiritually. Susan's leader would need to help her avoid spiritual pride and consider all the other needs of the group. Prayer might not be the biggest need right now. Also, Susan might not be ready to teach yet; she has been through the material only once herself.

Focusing on the Big Picture

Jesus also prepared His disciples to balance their successes with a heavenly vantage point. After the disciples returned from a fruitful ministry assignment, Jesus acknowledged their enthusiasm. Then He equipped them by highlighting God's big picture; their names were written in heaven (see Luke 10:17-20).

6. Read Luke 10:17-20 in the margin. How would the assurance that your name was written in heaven — salvation — give you balance in ministry?

_____

_____

_____

_____

Equipping young adults for ministry means helping them have a kingdom perspective, that being the mission of making disciples. Disappointment is inevitable, but if disciples are trained to expect resistance and thanklessness and are reminded that they serve God not people, their disappointments won't stop them. Disciple-makers can also prepare young adults so that they won't be swept away by people's praise. That way they can stay on target and grow as disciples who love God and people and serve both.

Review

- Equipping spiritual young adults to serve requires preparing them to remain balanced when disappointment or success occurs.
- Balance is found when we focus on God's bigger picture of our salvation and on building His kingdom.

day 3 PROVIDING MINISTRY OPPORTUNITIES

Intentional leaders must give disciples a place to serve and grow as they mature into the stage of spiritual young adult. We call this providing ministry opportunities. After disciple-makers see a heart change from self to others, they know that the disciple is moving to the young adult stage. It is time to further equip that person for ministry by giving him or her greater opportunities to serve. The end goal is to release young adults to serve on their own.

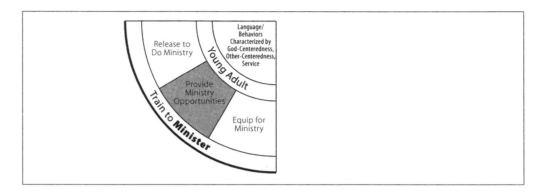

Luke 9:1-11 tells about Jesus sending His disciples out to preach the gospel in neighboring villages. They proclaimed the message wherever they were allowed, served the people by healing their illnesses, and cast out demons. But Jesus did not leave them to minister alone; they still needed His coaching. When they retuned, He listened to their report of what they had done.

1. What do you think Jesus talked about with the disciples when they returned? Circle your answers.

    A. How nice the weather had been
    B. What it was like to be rejected by some and accepted by others
    C. What it was like to proclaim the kingdom message
    D. How much money they made
    E. The meaning behind His teaching about the harvest
    F. What it was like to trust in God's provision

Jesus provided multiple ways for the disciples to participate in ministry. Sometimes He sent them to help others, other times they served food to crowds, and still other times they preached publicly. His disciples were allowed to get in the game. He did not simply teach and expect them to learn sitting on the bench nor did He abandon them to themselves. We think Jesus probably talked with them about B, C, E, and F when they returned.

See One, Do One, Teach One

A doctor reported that the phrase used in his medical training was "See one, do one, then teach one." In other words, his training began with watching a procedure. Next, he was allowed to participate in the procedure under supervision. Finally, when he was experienced, he began teaching someone else. Maybe the medical school got this pattern from Jesus? In any case, a spiritual young adult will grow in ministry with this approach.

2. Let's apply this concept. What ministry opportunities would be best for you personally to use a "See one, do one, teach one" approach?

☐ Leading a small group
☐ Teaching a Bible class
☐ Helping out in youth group
☐ Serving in the children's Sunday school with you
☐ Preparing and delivering meals for hurting families
☐ Making a hospital visit
☐ Other _____

3. Write out two examples of "See one, do one, teach one" for a ministry you would train a disciple to do. Break down a service opportunity into the equipping sequence of "See one, do one, teach one."

Here are some examples:

Leading Small Group	
See One	Invite a disciple to see how you prepare for a group and watch you lead the session.
Do One	Invite the disciple to lead a group session under your supervision and then with you gone.
Teach One	Invite the disciple to show another group member how to prepare and lead a group session.
Shepherding Group Members	
See One	Take the disciple with you as you connect with an absent member by calling the person, visiting his or her home, or meeting the individual for coffee.
Do One	Assign the disciple the task of connecting with another missing member of the group that week.
Teach One	Have the disciple teach another group member how to connect with a missing group member during the week.

Your turn:

See One	
Do One	
Teach One	
See One	
Do One	
Teach One	

Serving the Community

The word *ministry* is often too narrowly defined as church programs, such as Sunday school, youth ministry, and so forth. The New Testament concept of ministry included many things: making clothes for poor people (see Acts 9:36-42), serving food to widows (see Acts 6:1-6), and washing people's feet (see 1 Timothy 5:10), to name a few. Repairing a sink, watching children so parents can go on a date, and mowing a lawn are all ministries and can be used to help spiritual young adults mature.

As a way of instilling a ministry mindset, we set aside a Saturday just before Christmas for all the small groups at Real Life to serve in their communities. Some of the groups rake leaves or shovel snow. Others paint rooms and clean homes. One team goes around to all the tire stores to offer hot drinks and snacks to employees who are changing tires in the cold. All of these are ways of doing ministry. We call the day "Presence." This ministry helps people in our community, but it also helps spiritual young adults see ministry they can do outside of the church's walls and programs. Remember, Matthew 28:18-20 says to go to the world. Ministry happens in the church and in the world. Use every occasion as an opportunity to make disciples.

How have opportunities to "get in the game" of ministry impacted your growth?

Review

- Intentional leaders provide specific opportunities for disciples to get involved in ministry.
- A process of "See one, do one, teach one" helps spiritual young adults grow.
- Lead your disciples to serve in the church and the community.

RELEASED TO DO MINISTRY

day 4

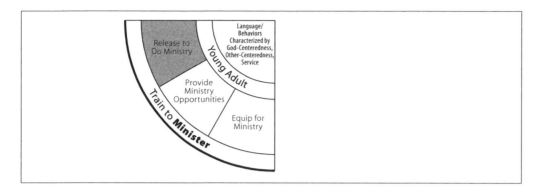

Releasing disciples for ministry helps prepare the disciples to lead. The coach must give them more responsibility and authority; only then will they take ownership and become confident and less dependent on the coach.

1. Read 2 Timothy 2:2 in the margin. Rewrite this verse as a note from a small-group leader to a new leader as that person starts his or her first group. What should the note say to do?

The things you have heard me say in the presence of many witnesses entrust to reliable men who will also be qualified to teach others.
(2 Timothy 2:2)

Dear _____,

(Signed) _____

Paul's words are for every disciple-maker. We do not pour our life into disciples to send them to the stands to watch. Disciple-making is a sacred trust. The disciple-maker obeys Christ by building an army for battle, not wax figures for a church museum.

Releasing People to Ministry

Acts 6:1-7 says that some widows in the church were being overlooked in the daily distribution of food. The apostles refused to stop their ministry of prayer and teaching the Word, but they did not ignore the problem. Instead, they released seven trusted leaders to minister to the neglected widows.

In those days when the number of disciples was increasing, the Grecian Jews among them complained against the Hebraic Jews because their widows were being overlooked in the daily distribution of food. So the Twelve gathered all the disciples together and said, "It would not be right for us to neglect the ministry of the word of God in order to wait on tables. Brothers, choose seven men from among you who are known to be full of the Spirit and wisdom. We will turn this responsibility over to them and will give our attention to prayer and the ministry of the word."

This proposal pleased the whole group. They chose Stephen, a man full of faith and of the Holy Spirit; also Philip, Procorus, Nicanor, Timon, Parmenas, and Nicolas from Antioch, a convert to Judaism. They presented these men to the apostles, who prayed and laid their hands on them.

(Acts 6:1-6)

Stephen, a man full of God's grace and power, did great wonders and miraculous signs among the people. Opposition arose, however, from members of the Synagogue of the Freedmen (as it was called)—Jews of Cyrene and Alexandria as well as the provinces of Cilicia and Asia. These men began to argue with Stephen, but they could not stand up against his wisdom or the Spirit by whom he spoke.

(Acts 6:8-10)

Those who had been scattered preached the word wherever they went. Philip went down to a city in Samaria and proclaimed the Christ there. When the crowds heard Philip and saw the miraculous signs he did, they all paid close attention to what he said. . . .

Philip, however, appeared at Azotus and traveled about, preaching the gospel in all the towns until he reached Caesarea.

(Acts 8:4-6,40)

2. Read Acts 6:1-6 in the margin. What happened to Stephen and Philip after they served the widows in the food line?

_____

_____

_____

_____

_____

3. What did Stephen do in Acts 6:8-10 (see the margin)?

_____

_____

_____

_____

_____

4. What did Philip do in Acts 8:4-6 and 8:40 (see the margin)?

_____

_____

_____

_____

_____

As we have seen, Jesus released the disciples to do ministry and help Him feed the five thousand. In Acts 6, we see the apostles following His example and releasing disciples to feed the widows. But next we see them working as disciple-makers on a mission to reach others. We will talk more about this next week, but for now, see the progression of how the apostles released these new disciples to do ministry.

Spiritual young adults still need coaching. They are free to minister but still need the encouragement and guidance of an intentional leader. They must learn how to set healthy boundaries and answer spiritual questions on their own. Let's look at each of these.

Healthy Boundaries

Disciples can't do it all. They need help to keep the main thing the mission of Christ. That is what the apostles were able to do in Acts 6. Reread Acts 6:1-6 and answer the following questions.

5. What boundary did the apostles set that required others to serve the widows?

_____

_____

_____

_____

_____

6. How do you think Stephen and Philip might have missed out if the apostles had not released them for ministry?

----

7. What do you think would have happened to the church if the apostles had refused to release these two for ministry?

The apostles literally said, "We should not stop serving the Word of God in order to serve food to widows." In other words, their priority was teaching the Word, so they gave the ministry task of serving the widows to the new disciples. Had the apostles not set this boundary, disciple-making for Stephen and Philip would have suffered, and the church would have slowed or even stopped in reaching the world for Jesus Christ.

Answering Spiritual Questions

Disciples are bound to encounter questions they have not thought of before. Disciples are learners. Don't rob them of the opportunity to find the answers on their own.

8. Which two of the following would most likely cause disciples to grow? Circle your answers.

    A. Being told the answer to a question they did not ask
    B. Searching the Bible to answer a question that is bugging them
    C. Being told to study a topic without a reason for studying it
    D. Being shown resources they can use to find biblical solutions

The two answers most likely to cause growth are B and D. Spiritual young adults have questions, but they are not like infants or children. They can find the answers for themselves.

Liz was struggling with a recent death in her family and had many questions. Melinda answered some, but then she showed Liz how to use a Bible concordance. Melinda turned Liz loose to study all the Bible passages about death. In the process, Liz found answers and learned more than she originally asked for. As Liz can tell you, one of the best ways for disciples to learn answers to spiritual questions is to do personal study.

Releasing disciples for ministry means handing off responsibility, setting boundaries, and using their questions to motivate them to find answers. All of this is done from a heart that loves and serves Jesus Christ.

Review
  • When we release disciples for ministry, we help them grow by setting healthy boundaries and learning how to find answers to questions.

day 5

A BREAK FOR REVIEW

One of our favorite sayings is "Repetition is the key to learning." You have been given a lot to think about in the last ten weeks. Today is dedicated to reviewing some of it before we move to the final phase of the discipleship process. Please complete the exercises from memory before looking back in the book to check.

Jesus' Command

The starting place is Jesus' command. During the time you have been studying and meeting with your small group, you may have seen other good endeavors that Christians have mistakenly put in the place of Jesus' command.

Here are a few we have seen:

- Offering humanitarian aid
- Providing access to Christian education
- Helping people achieve financial prosperity
- Training families to stay together

These are all good things and can surely happen in the context of fulfilling Jesus' command, but what was His command?

1. Fill in the blanks from memory. This was covered in week 1, day 1.

    Jesus commanded us to go into the world and _____
    _____ of every nation.

2. Three other action words show us what is entailed in obeying that command.

    To make disciples, we must be _____, _____,
    and _____.

3. How has your understanding of this command changed over the last ten weeks?

_____

_____

_____

_____

_____

_____

Definition of Disciple

Having the same goal in mind is essential for any team to succeed. People define what a disciple is in many ways. We took our definition from Jesus' call to the first disciples (see Matthew 4:19).

4. Fill in the blanks from memory:

A disciple is one who is _____ Jesus.

_____

_____

_____

A disciple is one who is being _____ by Jesus.

_____

_____

_____

A disciple is one who is _____ to the _____ of Jesus.

_____

_____

_____

5. Under each definition above, write what part of the disciple is being affected.

If you are not confident about what you wrote, go back to week 2 to check your answers.

6. How have these definitions of a disciple affected you over the course of this study?

_____

_____

_____

Discipleship Journey

7. Write the correct key to this journey below:

I_____ | R_____ | R_____ |
L_____ | E_____ | P_____ | = Disciples

8. In your own words, write a brief definition of each key to the discipleship journey.

- IL –

_____

_____

- RE –

  ....

  ....

- RP –

  ....

  ....

9. From these teachings, which one have you found most helpful? Share this with your group this week.

....

....

....

....

10. What does that principle look like lived out in your day-to-day discipleship?

....

....

....

....

disciple: being intentional with spiritual parents

The **disciple** phase of SCMD matches up well with the stage of spiritual parent. Let's look at the transition from the **ministry** phase to the **disciple** phase by comparing two disciples and their stages of maturity.

MAKING THE TRANSITION TO PARENTHOOD

day 1

Michael has participated in numerous Bible studies and ministry seminars since he became a Christian. Over the last ten years, he has read his Bible repeatedly from cover to cover and developed clear defenses for the Christian faith. He loves to study and discuss God's Word. His resource library continues to grow, and he has become somewhat of a "go-to guy" for people who have questions about the Bible. He is kind and humble and enjoys his special ministry of explaining Scripture to others.

1. Do you know anyone like Michael? If you do, write down that person's name.

Julie has grown by leaps and bounds since she joined a small group. She is a first-generation Christian who has grown through the intentional investment of her leader. In the last month, Julie realized that Christ's mission is hindered more by people *not* making disciples than anything else. She enjoys her ministry of teaching in the three-year-olds' class; however, she has become aware of what Christ's mission is. If she does not make disciples who can in turn make other disciples, she will fail to complete the work God has given her to do.

2. Mark an "M" by the characteristics you think fit Michael and a "J" by the ones that fit Julie. Write both letters if you think they fit both people.

    ____ Believes service to others is vital to a disciple's growth
    ____ Is well connected in a relational environment
    ____ Sees the need to be intentional about a person's spiritual growth
    ____ Measures spiritual maturity by the ability to explain the Bible
    ____ Likes to discuss and debate ideas pertaining to the Bible
    ____ Thinks discipleship primarily consists of Bible experts explaining God's Word
    ____ Sees ministry as done best by a team, not an individual
    ____ Feels an urgency to reproduce disciples who can disciple others

Though these descriptions are short, they can tell us whether Julie and Michael are ready to become spiritual parents and enter the **disciple** phase of the process.

3. Which one of the two do you think is most likely transitioning from being a spiritual young adult to a spiritual parent and why?

_____

_____

_____

_____

_____

There are clear signs that Julie may be making the transition, but not for Michael. Too often people assume that Bible knowledge alone is the best predictor of spiritual maturity. We emphatically believe that knowing your Bible is necessary for disciple; however, knowing all about it and doing little to intentionally make disciples is not a characteristic of a spiritual parent. Characteristics D, E, and F primarily fit Michael and are not indicators of a transition to spiritual parenthood.

4. Why do you think this stage uses the term spiritual parent instead of spiritual adult? Circle the letter of the reason you think is correct.

    A. Spiritual adult indicates leadership only
    B. Spiritual parent indicates the ability to reproduce and raise up disciples
    C. Spiritual adult is not a hip-enough title
    D. Spiritual adult sounds prideful
    E. Spiritual parent sounds more friendly

The ability to reproduce and raise up disciples is one of the primary indicators of a spiritual parent. B is the correct answer.

5. A disciple who is ready to become a spiritual parent demonstrates the characteristics below. In each space, write the letter of the following statements that best reflects whether you have that characteristic.

    A. I don't demonstrate this characteristic.
    B. I am developing this characteristic.
    C. I think my life reflects this characteristic.

    ____ Is ready and capable to reproduce disciples who can disciple others
    ____ Understands what it means to be intentional
    ____ Sees the greater mission to the world and the future
    ____ Has dependable relationships to support the person as he or she makes disciples
    ____ Has an experience-based understanding of the stages of spiritual growth
    ____ Is able to make connections from the stages of spiritual growth to the SCMD process by reflecting on his or her own growth and process

6. What characteristics do you need to develop in order to be ready to be a spiritual parent?

_____

_____

_____

_____

7. In which areas are you most ready to become a spiritual parent?

_____

_____

_____

Share your answers with the group this week.

Review

- The disciple phase of the SCMD process correlates with spiritual parenthood.
- There are many characteristics of spiritual parenthood, but most important is the ability to reproduce and raise up disciples who can make disciples.

day 2   EXPLAINING THE DISCIPLESHIP PROCESS

Dave was not discipled by an intentional leader in a relational environment with a reproducible process, but he loved the Lord and was committed to His mission. You could see it in his eyes and hear it in his voice. He was realizing how haphazard his discipleship had been, but he was putting it all together. As he talked with others about the discipleship process, each conversation helped him piece together how he had grown spiritually. This understanding made it possible for him to be intentional at disciple-making in the future.

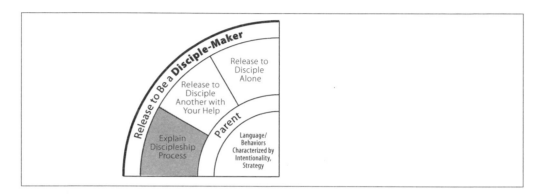

If you have been an intentional leader, you have taken the person you are discipling through the stages of growth and through a process. During this final phase of disciple-making, you need to explain both of these to your disciple so that he or she can be intentional about disciple-making as well. This explanation will help your disciple see how he or she has grown and identify which areas are weak and need work.

1. Identify the correct stage of the SCMD process next to each of Caleb's experiences described below. Use "S" for Share, "C" for Connection, and so forth.

    ____ Someone invited Caleb to a home group where they did Bible study and opened up about each other's struggles in order to pray for one another.

    ____ An elder in his church invited Caleb to go through a new member study for ten weeks right after he accepted Christ. Caleb had a lot of questions and the man took the time to answer them.

    ____ Caleb saw that the church needed help with the children's department, so he volunteered to serve there.

    ____ A guy at Caleb's work sat down with him to explain the gospel. Dave had never heard it before.

    ____ Caleb is now leading two groups of men in a Bible study about how to become more like Christ. He hopes they will be willing to do the same with other guys when they are done.

The correct answers are C, S, M, S, and D.

It is much easier to explain the process to someone who has been led through it intentionally. *Intentional* is the key word here. Jesus did not make disciples accidentally. As we said before, we believe that disciples are made best with an intentional process. For people to move into the *disciple phase* and become *spiritual parents,* they must have a clear explanation of the process.

2. Which of the following are benefits of having a clear explanation of the discipleship process, including the SCMD phases and the stages of spiritual growth?

    A. It provides a common language for others on the team.
    B. It is a good way to organize Bible verses.
    C. It clarifies what needs to happen when making disciples.
    D. It helps disciple-makers be intentional in their actions and assessments.
    E. It shows disciples what they will do someday with people they disciple.
    F. It highlights the importance of disciple-making by making it extremely complex.

We will review this more on the last day of this week, but for now you should have circled A, C, D, and E.

3. Did you ever have discipleship explained clearly to you? Why or why not?

4. As you reflect on the past ten weeks, how would you describe your personal growth? Check the stage you think you were in when we started our journey and place an "X" in the box next to the stage you think you are in now.

    ☐ Spiritually dead
    ☐ Spiritual infant
    ☐ Spiritual child
    ☐ Spiritual young adult
    ☐ Spiritual parent

5. If someone were to challenge where you think you are in the process, what evidence would you give to show that you are at the stage you selected?

Review

- The first thing to do in the disciple phase of the SCMD process is to explain the process clearly to disciples who are ready to be spiritual parents.
- An explanation of the process enables disciples to gain clarity so they can evaluate where they are in the process and become intentional in making disciples themselves.
- A clear explanation of the process provides a common language for everyone who is making disciples.

DISCIPLING TOGETHER

day 3

Brandon Guindon's first men's group was a challenge, but as the men began to grow relationally, several started to grow spiritually. God honored Brandon's efforts, and in about nine months the men in his group went from being spiritual infants to being spiritual young adults. They were speaking truth to each other, asking good questions, and applying God's Word to their lives. The Bible came alive to them, and Brandon saw positive changes in the way they viewed life and treated their families.

It was not long before Brandon knew that God wanted him to release these men to start other groups with his help. He intentionally coached and encouraged each leader. Before long, and not without trials, these men saw God at work in the new groups. Brandon celebrated their achievements and continued to coach them. Eventually they were discipling men whom Brandon would never have been able to reach.

New spiritual parents need help as they try on the responsibility of disciple-making solo.

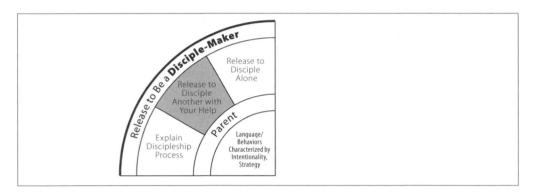

Last week in day 3 we used the idea of "See one, do one, teach one" as a template for providing ministry opportunities for spiritual young adults. Today we will apply a similar idea in the **disciple** phase of the SCMD process. We call this part "release to disciple another with your help." A good starting place is helping the disciples in this phase identify potential disciples.

Identifying Potential Disciples

God calls us to disciple our children (see Deuteronomy 6:5-9), so encourage your disciples to put their families at the top of the list. (They should be at the top of *your* list as well!)

As for discerning potential disciples outside the family, have your disciple begin with prayer. God is always at work around us, and we know His will is for disciples to be made. If we are praying and aligning our lives to the mission of Christ, God will show us who to disciple. Certainly if we lead someone to the Lord, God has committed that person to us to disciple.

Here is an example of how this happened for Brandon. He began to cross paths frequently with Brian, a young man in our church. During Brandon's devotions, God consistently put Brian on his heart, and Brandon felt God leading him to reach out to Brian by inviting him into a discipling relationship. Over the next few days, Brandon continued to pray about this, and then he set up a time to talk with Brian.

When they sat down together, Brandon asked Brian if he would be interested in meeting for discipleship. He said that their meetings would be focused intentionally on helping Brian grow in his walk with Christ. Brian said that he had been praying for several months, asking God to bring someone into his life to disciple him. At that moment, the relationship began.

Recognizing the Spiritually F.A.T.

Clearly, God was working in Brian's life, and clearly Brian was willing to be discipled. He was spiritually F.A.T.: **F**aithful, **A**vailable, and **T**eachable.

Each of these factors should be evident at each stage of growth, from spiritual infants through spiritual young adults. Looking for these F.A.T. qualities will help us discern whom to disciple.

1. Match the terms **Faithful (F)**, **Available (A)**, and **Teachable (T)** to their corresponding descriptions:

    ____ A person who is allocating time and priority to growing in his or her walk with Christ and in his or her relationships. The opposite would be someone who does not prioritize and value the importance of time together. *It does not work to disciple someone you have to beg or who is too busy to study outside your meeting.*
    ____ A person who is committed to the things of God. The opposite would be someone who is sporadic, impulsive, and unwilling. If someone is not serious about his or her faith, that person is not ready.
    ____ A person willing to learn and open to seeing new truth through honest questions. The opposite would be someone who is proud and argumentative at every turn.

    You should have labeled the descriptions in this order: Available, Faithful, and Teachable.

2. Read the following scenarios and circle the spiritually F.A.T. quality missing from the person you are hypothetically discipling.

    - **Jan** has been a Christian for about a year. She reads her Bible regularly, shares her faith at work, and attends two different churches, depending on her schedule. She is young and single and extremely busy. Jan has many questions about the Bible and loves to discuss God's Word and learn more. It took you two weeks to get a cup of coffee with her, and even when you finally met, she was fifteen minutes late. When you asked her to call you back, she lost your number. Had you not seen her at church, she might have waited a couple more weeks to get back to you.

Faithful	Available	Teachable

    - **Lou** has been a Christian for over ten years. Last week he confided to you that he felt stagnant in his spiritual life. He takes the Bible and his walk with Christ seriously and feels as though he needs help. When you met with him initially, he arrived ten minutes early. Lou had already thought of three different times during the week that he could clear his schedule. The first meeting felt more like an interrogation. Lou had questions about your credentials and seemed somewhat argumentative. Lou says, "There is nothing like a good debate."

Faithful	Available	Teachable

Both of these people need to be discipled, but they may not be ready and could be difficult to disciple intentionally. Jan is obviously too busy. You should have circled *available* as the missing component. Though Lou is *faithful* and *available*, he might not be *teachable*.

It may seem strange or awkward to walk up to someone like Brandon did with Brian, but Brandon recognized that Brian was spiritually F.A.T. If you are releasing a new spiritual parent to disciple another with your help, it begins with helping that person find the people they are going to disciple.

3. Circle below the letter corresponding to other details that you think new spiritual parents might need help with as they begin to disciple others in a small group:

A. Deciding what translation of the Bible to read for his or her personal devotions
B. Determining what activities and questions to use to create a relational environment
C. Finding a meeting time that works for everyone in the group
D. Assessing where each member of the group is in his or her spiritual maturity
E. Planning the weekly meeting
F. Compiling a phone and e-mail list of the group so they can contact each other during the week
G. Picking a T-shirt design that everyone likes and will wear as a way to identify that he or she is part of that particular small group
H. Putting together a snack schedule

You should have circled all the letters except for A and G.

4. What other details might a new disciple-maker need your help with?

_____

_____

_____

_____

_____

Share your list with your group this week, and discuss specific ways you can help a new disciple-maker succeed.

Review

- A new disciple-maker will need help getting started.
- Finding people to disciple is best done by determining who is spiritually F.A.T.: Faithful, Available, and Teachable.
- The new disciple-maker may need help with other details as well, ranging from planning the meetings to assessing where people are in their spiritual growth stages.

RELEASING TO DISCIPLE ALONE

day 4

The final part of the **disciple** phase is releasing them to disciple alone.

Intentional leaders recognize the value and importance of this handoff. They put into place a plan to effectively release someone to make disciples by explaining the process of discipleship and then clearly transferring that responsibility. As parents, we make this transfer with our children. We want them to be able to parent their own kids. That is the natural process of life.

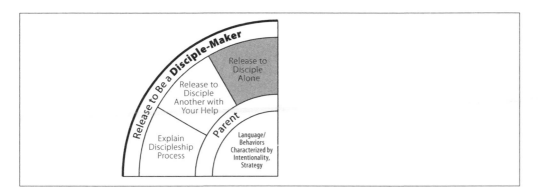

Jesus Released His Disciples

When Jesus had completed His work of making the Twelve into disciple-makers, He released them. He commanded us to do the same in what is called the Great Commission (see Matthew 28:18-20). When Jesus released His disciples, they no longer needed specific instructions and limited objectives, as their training was complete. They were ready to do what they had been trained to do. When Jesus gave them the Great Commission, they just needed the command, vision, and assurance that He would be with them always.

The time has come. Your disciple is ready. Disciple-making is no longer something he or she does; it is becoming who that disciple is. The Great Commission is now for your disciple as well, and you must transfer the responsibility of disciple-making over to him or her. Your disciple, in turn, must transfer his or her dependence on you to Jesus, who promised to be with us always.

Acknowledgment and Recognition

When disciple-makers release spiritual parents, the clear transfer of responsibility does two things:

- It changes the way disciples look at the ministry they have just taken on. They have assumed a responsibility and will be held accountable for it by Christ (see Luke 12:48; 2 Corinthians 5:10).
- It gives them confidence that they will be supported when circumstances demand it.

As we commission spiritual parents to their ministry, they become our peers in disciple-making. They are now making disciples without depending on our direct leadership. We move out of the way so these new spiritual parents can rely on the Holy Spirit for guidance. The message of John 15:1-15 makes this new dependency evident. We must get out of the way and allow God to work in the spiritual parents we are releasing. This creates healthy disciple-makers.

I am the true vine, and my Father is the gardener. He cuts off every branch in me that bears no fruit, while every branch that does bear fruit he prunes so that it will be even more fruitful. You are already clean because of the word I have spoken to you. Remain in me, and I will remain in you. No branch can bear fruit by itself; it must remain in the vine. Neither can you bear fruit unless you remain in me.

I am the vine; you are the branches. If a man remains in me and I in him, he will bear much fruit; apart from me you can do nothing. If anyone does not remain in me, he is like a branch that is thrown away and withers; such branches are picked up, thrown into the fire and burned. If you remain in me and my words remain in you, ask whatever you wish, and it will be given you. This is to my Father's glory, that you bear much fruit, showing yourselves to be my disciples.
(John 15:1-8)

1. Read John 15:1-8 in the margin. From this passage, what does Jesus say is vitally important for disciple-makers?

2. What helps you the most to maintain a healthy connection to Jesus?

3. How will you provide those supports for the disciple-makers that you release?

4. What fears do you think your disciples might have when you release them to go out and make disciples?

5. What could you do to help relieve those fears?

6. Answer each of the following questions by focusing on the word in bold letters.

• What will you intentionally do to **prepare** a spiritual parent to be released to make disciples?

- What will you intentionally do to **release** the spiritual parent?

Discuss your answers in the small-group session. To effectively send out spiritual parents, intentional leaders need to think through the actual process of letting them go. If we keep these questions in mind throughout the discipleship process, we will continue to generate ideas for releasing spiritual parents effectively.

Review

- The final action of the disciple phase is to release the individual to disciple alone.
- New disciple-makers accept Matthew 28:18-20 as a personal commission from Jesus.
- This release highlights the importance of the disciple-maker's connection to Christ.

day 5

MAINTAINING RELATIONSHIPS AMONG SPIRITUAL PARENTS

The key to learning is repetition. Let's take some time to review the discipleship wheel to ensure that you are clear on this process and can use the wheel as a tool.

1. Below is a blank discipleship wheel. How much of it can you fill from memory? Look back in the manual as you need to.

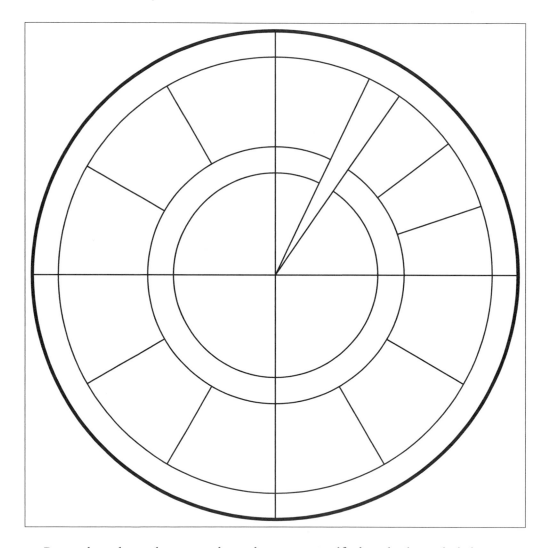

Remember, the tool never replaces the process itself; the wheel simply helps us put words and a picture to the discipleship process Jesus laid out for His disciples. This is a tool to help you become more intentional as you prepare and release disciples.

Relating to Those You Release

When you release spiritual parents, some things about your relationship must change. You must change how you view them. You are no longer responsible for them. You are releasing them to make their own decisions without depending on you. Instead, they are to rely on God's Word and His Spirit for guidance.

2. What would you do if a spiritual parent you had released came to you with a question about something he or should already know the answer for?

You should assure the spiritual parent that he or she already knows the answer and then ask the person to tell you what he or she thinks it is. Do not jump in and give the answer. This spiritual parent is looking for assurance and support and needs you to help him or her get that from God and from experience instead of always depending on you.

3. What would you do if the person can't come up with the answer?

We think you should help the person discover the answer with you. Take the time, search the Bible, and ask others you trust. It is healthy for the new parent to see that you are still learning too.

4. How should you respond if a spiritual parent makes a mistake?

When spiritual parents make mistakes—and they will—allow them to experience the consequences. Don't be a mother hen. Allow them to learn and improve without your monitoring their every move. Instead, encourage them by telling them about a mistake you made and how you learned from it and grew.

However, when you release disciples to be spiritual parents, some things should stay the same. For one, you should not stop affirming them and praising them. You must encourage them when they do well, especially if they are having problems. Virtually no mistake is fatal, and the fact that they are in there swinging deserves some encouragement. You did not release them from your relationship and your support, even though they are no longer dependent on you.

You also need to keep your relationship up-to-date and fresh. Make a mutual accountability commitment.

5. How can you keep your relationships fresh with the spiritual parents you have released to make disciples?

_____

_____

_____

_____

_____

Some of our best friends are people we have discipled. Even though we and our former disciples are making new disciples and forging new relationships, we still maintain our longtime relationships with each other.

All of us need friends we can call on to keep us accountable and give us strength and encouragement. All of us need long-term friends who really know us and can look into our eyes and call us on things that need our attention. We *must* manage our lives in a way that enables us to maintain certain fellow disciple-maker relationships.

Greet Priscilla and Aquila, my fellow workers in Christ Jesus.
(Romans 16:3)

Greet Urbanus, our fellow worker in Christ, and my dear friend Stachys.
(Romans 16:9)

Timothy, my fellow worker, sends his greetings to you, as do Lucius, Jason and Sosipater, my relatives.
(Romans 16:21)

We are God's fellow workers; you are God's field, God's building.
(1 Corinthians 3:9)

Not that we lord it over your faith, but we work with you for your joy, because it is by faith you stand firm.
(2 Corinthians 1:24)

6. Read the verses in the margin (Romans 16:3,9,21; 1 Corinthians 3:9; 2 Corinthians 1:24) and place a checkmark by the statements that are themes from the verses:

☐ Once you release a disciple, you should break close ties with that person.
☐ You cannot remain friends with those who become spiritual parents.
☐ The spiritual parents you release are your co-laborers in the mission of discipleship.
☐ The discipleship process results in disciple-makers working together.
☐ Disciple-makers keep in communication with people they have released.

In the verses, we can see how Paul uses such statements as *fellow workers* and *working together*. You should have checked the last three statements.

Review
- We want to maintain relationships with those we release to make disciples.
- Spiritual parents cannot remain healthy if they are alone.
- The disciple-maker becomes a co-laborer with the disciple-maker he or she has released.

one necessary tool: a small-group curriculum

Wow, you made it to the end! While this training manual is a resource you can refer back to as you go along, God has also given you another great resource: the group of people who joined you for this study.

We saved this section until the end because you needed to understand *how* to make disciples. During our last week together, we want to give you one essential tool for disciple-making: the curriculum we use in our small groups at Real Life Ministries.

WHY BIBLE STORYING?

day 1

Curriculum is simply a tool in the hands of disciple-makers. If you have come this far with us, you know that no curriculum in itself is going to make disciples. One discipling method we like to use is called *Bible storying*, which means orally telling the stories of the Bible based on chronological order, themes, needs of the audience, and so on. Telling a story is not the same as reading it. (You can see a Bible-storying demonstration on the web at www.dna-21.org.)

When we began using Bible storying in our small groups, some people questioned the decision. Even some of our own leaders hesitated. Here is why we made the change.

Jesus' and the Early Church's Example

1. Read the story Jesus told in Matthew 13:34 in the margin. Put a checkmark by the reasons you think Jesus told stories as He made disciples.

> *Jesus spoke all these things to the crowd in parables; he did not say anything to them without using a parable.*
>
> *(Matthew 13:34)*

□ Because most of the people of His day were illiterate
□ So that those He was teaching would understand and remember
□ To keep those who refused to believe from understanding
□ Because He was transforming their worldview
□ Because God wired us to like stories
□ Because He was mostly talking to children

You should have put a checkmark next to all but the last one. How did you do?

Nearly all of the people of Jesus' era were illiterate, so He needed to use oral teaching methods. Though our culture is certainly much more literate than the New Testament world, many people today do not prefer to learn by reading. Avery Willis reports that almost 60 percent of Americans never read another book after high school.

Storying also has benefits for those who are highly educated. Stories convey a message in a way that everyone can remember, and they make the point. However, Jesus said He also hid the truth in stories from those who were hard-hearted (see Matthew13:11-13).

We see the world through the stories of our lives and the lives of others. The best way to transform one's worldview is by renewing the mind through the stories found in God's Word (see Romans 12:2). Over time, stories eat away at false beliefs and validate the truth.

We are not saying you shouldn't teach directly from Scripture. Peter, Paul, and other writers of the New Testament quoted and used the Old Testament to teach God's truth. However, we are saying that storying God's Word can be an invaluable tool in the discipleship process and it covers most of the truth in a natural way.

Early Christians only had a few Old Testament scrolls. They did not have a written New Testament, and so they had to tell accurate stories about what Jesus did and taught (see Acts 1:1). The writers of the New Testament quoted and used the Old Testament to teach God's truth as they built their theology on stories of Jesus and the inspired revelations from God.

These things happened to them as examples and were written down as warnings for us, on whom the fulfillment of the ages has come. So, if you think you are standing firm, be careful that you don't fall!
(1 Corinthians 10:11-12)

2. Read 1 Corinthians 10:11-12 in the margin. Paul had just told his readers some of Israel's stories. According to this Scripture, why did God have these stories written down for us?

_____

_____

_____

_____

You should have written that these stories are examples of what to do and what not to do.

It Works

Here is how one small-group leader described the first time he used Bible storying in his small group.

> I was so nervous about trying this approach. I over-prepared and memorized way too much of the story. But once I jumped into telling it, I noticed immediately that people were engaged. What amazed me was that people were listening as though they had never heard the story, although I knew they had because we had studied it before.
>
> I had asked them to listen carefully so they could tell the story back to me. When I finished, people who never spoke up before began to help retell the story. The whole group got involved. I sat there almost as an observer while the group self-corrected the story. I had spent so many years mastering all kinds of curriculum, and, to be honest, this approach seemed way too easy. But it was incredible to see how effective it was. We have seen more transformation in people's lives because of storying than any other curriculum we have ever used.

Makes It Easy to Apply Truth to Real-Life Situations

One seven-year-old girl overheard her parents discussing someone's daughter who was "lost." She blurted out, "Dad, who lost their daughter?" Her father explained that the girl was not physically lost but was choosing not to follow Jesus.

She said, "Dad, that girl is like Peter. She is looking at the waves, and anyone that doesn't keep their eyes on Jesus will sink." Two weeks before, this girl had heard her dad recount the story about Peter walking on water (see Matthew 14:22-33).

If a seven-year-old can learn a Bible story, retell it accurately, and make direct life application, then people at all stages of spiritual growth can use this tool.

3. Write about an experience you had that confirms how storying makes application easier.

_____

_____

_____

_____

_____

_____

Encourages Dialogue

In the natural dialogue that follows the story, the intentional leader has a chance to listen for "phrases from the stage" because he or she is not doing all the talking. Such listening enables the leader to better identify where people are in the reproducible process. We will spend day 4 on this point.

More People Have a Chance to Get in the Game

People quickly see that one doesn't have to be an expert to tell a story. Just tell the story, ask questions, and apply the reproducible process for making disciples.

Review

- Your turn. Why use Bible storying?

1. _____

2. _____

3. _____

4. _____

5. _____

6. _____

day 2

A STORYING SESSION

Today we want to take you to one of our home groups so you can see how Bible storying plays out. We hope that you had the opportunity to watch a demonstration on the www .learningtosoar.org website. That should bring it to life for you. We've tried to capture a Real Life home-group session below. Let's drop in.

Setting the Stage

As people arrive at the home, they're greeted warmly by Rob and Jill. There are snacks and coffee in the kitchen, and people gather to catch up on the past week. One of the parents leads the children to another room to see an approved video, play some games, or have a storying session themselves on a child's level.

After everyone arrives, Rob welcomes the people, introduces those who are new, and then leads the group in discussing their experiences of the week and takes prayer requests.

1. What are some things Rob did (or could do) to create a relational environment in the group?

Introducing the Story

After prayer, Rob starts the storying session. First, he asks for volunteers to tell what happened when they retold last week's story to someone. Everyone laughs at some of the reactions and slipups; they also rejoice to hear some breakthroughs with people. Rob asks volunteers to tell the main thing they learned from applying the story to their own lives.

At that point, Rob tells the group about coming to a small group for the first time and realizing how far he was from a discipleship lifestyle. He asks if anyone else has had a similar experience. A couple of people tell similar stories, and by the time they are done, everyone is considering the question personally.

Rob says, "Our story tonight is found in Luke 5:1-11, but I ask you to just listen to it as a story. This is the story about Jesus calling Peter and his friends to leave their fishing business and follow Him. Do you remember any of the stories about these men's relationships with Jesus leading up to this story?" Several talk about John's disciples following Jesus, going to the Cana wedding feast, and going to the synagogue and to Peter's house the night before.

Rob goes on to say, "As I tell the story, listen carefully for the answers to these two questions: *What did it mean to Peter for Jesus to get into his boat?* and *Why did Peter ask Jesus to leave him?*"

2. How did Rob use the previous week's story, his personal experience, and questions to connect the group in this week's introduction to the story?

Rob linked this story with the chronological sequence of what happened before and helped the group see that Jesus had already been involved in the disciples' lives before He gave this new challenge.

Telling the Story

Rob begins by saying, "Here is the story from God's Word." His Bible is open, but he doesn't look at it and he tells us to close our Bibles and listen to it as a story. He looks each person in the eye as he tells the story simply but accurately. Several of the people sit on the edge of their seats, leaning forward, taking in every word. When he finishes, he says, "That's the story from God's Word." It must have taken not three to five minutes to tell the story. Rob doesn't add any personal comments or explanation to the story.

3. What struck you as unique about the way Rob told the story?

You may have mentioned several things, but we like the simplicity and accuracy. The key is asking questions rather than telling the meaning or application.

Rebuilding the Story

Head	Heart	Hands
What?	Why?	How?
What?	So what?	Now what?
Observations	Implications/interpretations	Application

Rob uses the chart above to ask questions. He begins with "head" questions, which deal with just the facts of the story: who, what, when, where, and how. He saves the "why" questions until the next series of questions. His questions help the group retell the story, and everyone can participate. Then he uses the "heart" questions to guide the group in talking about what the story meant. Lastly he asks "hands" questions to help the members apply the story to their lives.

Everyone seems to identify with the disciples' experience. Rob asks for a volunteer to retell the story, and the group enthusiastically supports Marcie when she does. They have fun as they help fill in what she left out.

4. What did Rob do to get the people to discuss the story?

_____
_____
_____
_____
_____
_____

The key is asking questions rather than telling what the story means and how it applies.

Follow Through

Rob asks everyone in the group to tell the story at work, to someone in their family, or to an acquaintance during the coming week. He also asks for a volunteer to tell the next story in the series. Jerry volunteers easily. After all, it's not intimidating to retell a story. We all go home with a story firmly in our hearts and a desire to be Christ's disciples.

5. How did Rob help the people use the story the following week?

_____
_____
_____
_____
_____
_____

If you are unsure of the answers for today's questions, don't worry. We will keep learning more about Bible storying throughout week 12 and see a live example of it actually done in your small-group time. Simple enough, huh? You can get a more complete description and training in *Truth That Sticks: How to Communicate Velcro Truth in a Teflon World* (NavPress, 2010). Avery demonstrates how to tell this specific story (Luke 5:1-11) at www.learningtosoar.org.

Review

- Hook the group into the story with questions that raise interest.
- Tell the story as accurately as you can.
- Ask questions to get people to talk about the story.
- "Hands" questions help people follow through with application.

HOW TO USE BIBLE STORIES TO MAKE DISCIPLES

day 3

Yesterday you read a brief description of how a storying session works. Today we want to discuss what Rob did to make it work.

Introducing the Story

An easy way to remember how to introduce the story is to think of an upside-down question mark, which looks like a hook (⸮). Ask questions that hook your listeners instead of making statements. If questions are hooks, then statements of fact would look like an explanation mark, or a club (!).

A good story introduction uses three hooks related to the past, present, and future.

The "Past" Hook helps get the group talking about their experiences with the previous week's story.

1. Circle the letters for the questions that will get people to talk about the previous week's story:

    a. What happened when you told last week's story to someone else?
    b. Did you know the story before last week?
    c. How did God use the story in your life this week?
    d. Can you tell all the stories up to now?

Rob brought his group on board by asking questions *a* and *c*.

The "Present" Hook helps you relate to the needs of the members by raising the issue in today's story.

2. Circle the letters for the statements that would help the group relate to the issue in the story:

    a. A mini-devotional on why we need to be disciples and follow Jesus
    b. A personal experience about being challenged to be a disciple
    c. Starting the story with no warm-up
    d. Asking others to tell of a similar experience
    e. Getting the group to discuss the issue so they are involved

Rob hooked them with his personal story and got them to relate theirs so they could discuss what it means to be a disciple, which was the issue in the story. He did not launch right into the Bible story until group members had identified a personal need the story would speak to. Letters *b*, *d*, and *e* are correct.

The "Future" Hook involves asking a couple of questions so the group has to listen for the answers in the story you are about to tell.

3. Check the questions Rob asked:

    ☐ He asked if they had ever heard the story before.
    ☐ He asked fact questions.
    ☐ He asked questions that made them think.
    ☐ He asked simple questions they could remember.

Rob asked two simple questions about how the group would interpret events in the story. He did not just ask about the facts of the story, although it would have been okay to do so.

4. Are you able to tell a friend how to introduce a Bible story in a group with these three hooks? If not, review the process again before moving on.

Telling the Story

5. Circle the letters corresponding to what Rob did as he told the story.

    a. He asked someone to read the story aloud first.
    b. He told people to check the story in their Bibles as he told it.
    c. He looked people in the eyes as he told it.
    d. He opened his Bible but didn't read or look at it.
    e. He explained the fishing habits of fishermen at the Sea of Galilee.
    f. He told the story as accurately as he could without memorizing it.
    g. He did not add any personal comments about the story, the setting, or the meaning.
    h. He said, "Here is the story from God's Word" at the beginning.
    i. He urged the members to be disciples.
    j. He closed his Bible at the end and said, "That was the story from God's Word."

You should have circled *c, d, f, g, h,* and *j.*

Rob began the story by opening his Bible and saying, "This is the story from God's Word." This statement is important because it gives the story authority. It is not a fairy tale or a story he made up; it is God's Word. Rob told the story as accurately as he could remember, without using notes or reading directly from his Bible. The story should be told from memory and with your heart, as if you are retelling the miracle of watching your child's birth. Try not to recite the story while staring straight ahead. Maintain eye contact with your audience. Use positive body language, such as sitting forward in your chair, leaning into the audience, and using hand motions. Rob also avoided adding his personal comments. It is important for the hearers to hear God's Word rather than our opinions or interpretations at this point. We'll get to them later. He closed his Bible at the end to show that he had finished the story and that the group would now discuss it.

How do you learn to tell the story without looking at your Bible or notes? Here are several suggestions.

6. Underline the ways you think will help you learn to tell a Bible story:

- Read the story over and over until it begins to flow.
- Read different translations to identify the key elements of the story.
- Try to tell the story, and then check to see what you left out or added.
- Picture the story in scenes and think of them as a movie playing in your mind.
- Listen to a recording of the story until you can repeat it in your own words.
- Notice the transitions where you might forget what comes next and be sure you have a statement to get you from one scene to the next.
- Practice telling the story in private.
- Ask others to listen to you tell the story while they check their Bibles.
- Practice telling the story to anyone who will listen.
- Record yourself telling the story and listen to see if you told it accurately and interestingly.
- Think through the story or tell it from the perspective of each of the characters so you get "inside the story."

7. Try telling Luke 5:1-11 to your family and friends. You'll get better and better as you practice, and what you say will come out as a story just as it would if you were telling about your children or a hunting trip.

Rebuilding the Story: "Head" Questions

This process has two purposes. First, if the group knows they will be rebuilding the story after you tell it, they will pay closer attention and be more invested. Second, their retelling of the story solidifies it in their minds in chronological order. Your job is to guide them through by asking such questions as "So where does the story start?" "What happened next?" "What did she say in the story?" "After that, where did they go?"

This questioning helps the group walk through the story and self-correct. If someone adds something to the story, the group (or you as the leader) can correct the error. Make sure to praise the audience continuously for correct answers and sharing what they remember. Have fun with mistakes rather than make people feel that they messed up.

Read the Story Aloud

At this point, you can have the group open their Bibles and ask someone to volunteer to read the story out loud. Do not specify someone to read aloud. That can intimidate people. Ask for volunteers; if you wait patiently, someone will step forward.

As the story is read, the group has the experience of witnessing again the authority of the story. Ask the group to look for things you may have left out or added to the story when you told it. This ensures we preserve the accuracy of Scripture and also helps the audience feel that you do not have to be perfect to tell the story.

Review
- Hook your group, using questions to talk about the past, present, and future.
- Learn your message as a story instead of memorizing it word for word.
- Rebuild the story by having the group retell it.
- Read the story aloud from God's Word.

day 4　　THE PHRASE FROM THE STAGE

Each Christian has a spiritual-growth story that spans from new birth to maturity. Your personal spiritual-growth story tells your progress in the Christian life and how well you align with God's story. As we grow in Christlikeness, it is a story worth telling!

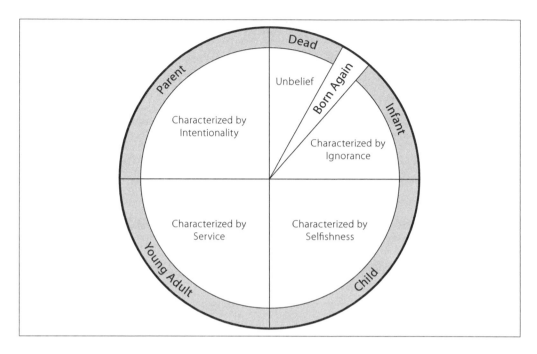

One of the remarkable things about storying in a group is that people at all the stages of development can grow at their own pace, much like children grow in a family.

Bible storying is important because by creating an atmosphere in which stories are told and questions are asked, intentional leaders can know where people are by what they say, and know what they need to do to help people grow to the next stage. If you know the "share, connect, minister, disciple" process and "the phrase from the stage," you know where people are by their comments and you can help them. When you use questions, people open up and you can know what they know about God, what they understand, and what they are doing with the information.

Spiritually Dead: Characterized by Unbelief

From an evangelical point of view, 90 percent of the world's population claims not to have a personal relationship with Christ. Another 20 percent calls themselves Christians but would not be considered evangelicals or born again.[5] We all start out as unbelievers and fit Paul's description: "You were dead in your transgressions and sins" (Ephesians 2:1).

The task at this stage is for the intentional discipleship leader and group members to share the gospel with the unbeliever. The beautiful thing about storying to unbelievers is that it gives them an interesting, easy way to grasp the gospel. When storying occurs in a relational group with an intentional leader, unbelievers have a place to discover God's plan for their lives.

These statements could be said by a spiritually dead person:

- "I think that I will get to heaven because I am as good as the next person."
- "I don't believe there is a God."
- "God is just a crutch."
- "There are many ways to get to God."
- "A good person gets to go to heaven, a bad person goes to hell."
- "I am a Christian because I go to church and I am a good person."
- "There is no hell because God is a God of love."
- "There is no absolute right and wrong."
- "I don't know where I am going if I die."

Each of these statements could be made by a spiritually dead person and should alert us that this person is in the spiritually dead phase of growth. We know that we need time to share the gospel with him or her.

The Infant Stage: Characterized by Ignorance

In 1 Peter 2:2-3, we read, "Like newborn babies, crave pure spiritual milk, so that by it you may grow up in your salvation, now that you have tasted that the Lord is good." It is the job of the parent to be sure that the newborn baby has milk; it is the task of the leader and the group to build relationships with new believers and connect them to God's truth. New Christians in the infant stage need to be connected to a small group that will help them be connected to Christ on a regular basis through all the means available.

Here are some phrases that a spiritual infant is likely to say during the storying dialogue:

- "Why do I need to go to church regularly?"
- "I've been hurt by a lot of people, so it's just me and God. I don't need others."
- "I don't need anyone else, just me and Jesus."
- "If I pray and read my Bible, will I be good enough?"
- "I provide for my family. I don't have time for the church."
- "What should I do about my old friends who don't believe?"
- "I didn't know the Bible said that."
- "I know that Jesus is Lord and Savior, but is karma real?"
- "Does God let dead people, such as my grandma, visit us to give us messages from Him?"

We can begin to address these issues by sharing our lives with spiritual infants, sharing new truth that challenges them, and sharing new habits to help them progress in their spiritual lives.

The Child Stage: Characterized by Self-Centeredness

The apostle John calls Christians "children" (see 1 John 2:12-13). Repeatedly in 1 John he brings up the subject of relationships between these children (see 1:6; 2:9-11,19; 3:16-18; 4:7,11,20-21). One of a spiritual child's greatest needs is to belong to a family. Relationships are key to his or her growth. It is natural for disciples at this stage to be mostly concerned about themselves. Left to their natural self-centeredness, they will become stunted in their growth as disciples. God uses connection to a family to help a disciple see the needs of others. Listening to a person's responses to a Bible story will give clues to his or her maturity. Is he or she a spiritual child?

Here are some phrases that a spiritual child is likely to say during the storying dialogue:

- "I believe in Jesus, and I worship Him best in the woods, just me and Jesus."
- "Don't branch my group into two groups. It is comfortable for me right now."
- "This story doesn't seem to say anything to me."
- "I love my small group. Don't add any more people to it."
- "My small group is not taking care of my needs like they should."
- "I don't have anyone who is spending enough time with me."
- "I want to change the study to something I am interested in."
- "I am not being fed in this small group. I need a group that meets my needs better."
- "Pastor looked right at me and didn't even say hello."

Spiritual children need to be assured that they belong. At the same time, we challenge them to see the needs of others around them and consider that God may be calling them to serve others.

Young Adults: Characterized by Service

The apostle John wrote to the young men, "You are strong, and the word of God lives in you, and you have overcome the evil one" (1 John 2:14). Spiritual young adults are becoming "others-centered" and look out for others' needs.

Spiritual young adults choose to minister to others. Whether that service is working with others in the church or helping with a ministry for outsiders, they are no longer looking out for just themselves.

Here is a list of phrases characteristic of young adults:

- "I love my group, but there are others who need a group like this."
- "I think I could lead a group with a little help. I have three friends I have been witnessing to, and this group would be too big for them."
- "Look how many are at church today—it's awesome! I had to walk two blocks from the closest parking spot."
- "Randy and Rachel missed group, and I called to see if they are okay. Their kids have the flu, so can our group make meals for them? I'll start."
- "In my devotions, I came across something I have a question about."
- "I noticed that we don't have an old folks visitation team. Do you think I could be involved?"

At this point, you want to give spiritual young adults opportunities to try out ministries to discover what they want to focus on.

Parents: Characterized by Intentionality

At this stage, the person becomes more intentional about discipling others. These statements indicate a person is moving into the parent stage:

- "This guy at work asked me to explain the Bible to him. Pray for me."
- "We get to baptize someone from our small group tonight. When is the next 101 class? I want to get her plugged into ministry somewhere."
- "Our small group is going on a mission trip, and I have given each person a different responsibility."
- "I realize discipleship happens at home, too. Will you hold me accountable to spend time discipling my kids?"
- "I have a person in my small group who is passionate about children. Can you have the children's ministry people call me?"

People who say things similar to these statements are moving into the spiritual parent stage. The emphasis at this stage is reproduction. When disciples become parents, they are concerned not only about the growth of their own family (small group) but also the vitality of those around them (church) and those they must intentionally reach out to (evangelism and missions).

It's important to give spiritual parents a place "to play" and opportunities to begin discipling others. A spiritual parent is ready to lead a small group because he or she has experienced the entire reproducible process.

Review

- Christians grow through stages of spiritual growth.
- Our language will reveal which stage we are in.
- By just asking questions and listening, the intentional leader will be able to discern which stage a person is in.

day 5

GUIDING THE STORY IN THEIR HEADS, HEARTS, AND HANDS

Today we will cover asking good questions that facilitate discussions about the Bible story. This involves introducing and telling the story as well as helping the story find its way into each person's head, heart, and hands. Does that sound familiar?

Head	Heart	Hands
What?	Why?	How?
What?	So what?	Now what?
Observations	Implications/interpretations	Application

"Head" Questions

Remember that your job as a facilitator (a helper of learning) is to ask questions, keep the discussion going, and get members talking to one another. Asking questions about the facts of the story helps everyone feel capable of entering into the conversation. Keep asking people what happens next. If they skip something, ask them what happened before that. This can be a five- to ten-minute time of rebuilding the story in their minds so they remember it.

"Heart" Questions

Once the story is in their heads, move it to their hearts with "why" questions that get to the meaning or interpretation of the story. Let group members struggle with the meaning of the story without your interpretation. Ask open-ended questions instead of yes-or-no questions, which kill discussion. You might ask deeper questions that have no answer since they're not answered in the story. You might ask if anyone knows another story in the Bible that answers the question.

Here are some questions to ask to help members get inside the story and begin to think about its meaning:

- Why do you think he said that?
- Identify any problem, obstacle, barrier, or difficulty presented in the story. What is the problem?
- Is the problem solved? Has the obstacle, barrier, or difficulty been overcome? If so, how?
- What does this story tell us about God?
- What does this story tell us about people?
- Was anything in this story new to you?
- Do you have a question about anything in the story?
- What do you like about this story? What don't you like about this story?

Choose questions that get listeners involved in the meaning of the story. The group will also ask questions. Resist answering them yourself. Ask the one who asked the question what he or she thinks, or throw the question back to the group. Consider asking the group to find the answer and report back the following week.

The most difficult thing for teachers and preachers to overcome in Bible storying is the habit of interjecting their explanations during the telling of the story or during the discussion after the story has been told. Just yesterday, we heard about someone who is thinking of leaving a group because when the leader asks a question, he immediately proceeds to answer it. Everyone else in the group has to just sit and listen.

1. Why do you think leaders feel they have to give the answers?

_____

_____

_____

_____

_____

Many of us are afraid that people won't interpret the story correctly, or we just want to tell them what we know.

If someone gives an incorrect answer, ask the group to discuss the options and figure out the best interpretation. Unless you need to head off a heresy, let the members lead the group to an accurate interpretation. If they don't come anywhere near an accurate interpretation, you might speak up and give your interpretation. If people bring up controversial questions that don't relate to the story, tell them that you will be glad to talk with them privately but that you won't take group time to discuss the question. You might ask the person to look up the answer and report back the next week. As much as possible, stick to the story and how it applies to our lives.

2. Using what we've discussed, write down some key points you will want to develop as you learn to tell Bible stories.

_____

_____

_____

_____

"Hands" Questions

Once the "why" questions have helped the group understand the meaning of the story, move to the "hands" (application) questions. It is important to ask "how" questions that will help them apply the story to their lives.

The application questions are the ones that are most often ignored. Be bold enough to ask the hard questions. Hands-level change comes when we hear the story from God's Word and effective questions force us to look at our own lives in comparison to the story we just heard.

3. Go back to Luke 5:1-11, which you storied yesterday, and generate some follow-up questions you could use to go further.

Head:

1. _____

2. _____

Heart:

1. _____

2. _____

Hands:

1. _____

2. _____

Review

- Use "what" questions to get the story into their heads.
- Use "why" questions to get the story into their hearts.
- Use "how" questions to get the story into their hands.

We have come to the end of a twelve-week tour, but we hope your journey will continue. During the writing of this book, Avery Willis was diagnosed with a terminal illness, and now more than ever we feel the urgency to get the message of the gospel to the nations. Our intention continues to be obeying our Lord Jesus by fulfilling His command to make disciples. We have joined the ranks of Christians who have made disciples for two thousand years. Discipleship is the chain that links the ministry of Jesus to our future in heaven. You are a link in that chain. Be an intentional leader whom God uses to reconcile people to Himself. Make disciples. Join us as we count it a privilege to be used by God.

summary and profile of each stage of spiritual growth

General Characteristics of the Stage

Spiritual Stage	
Dead	Unbelieving
	Rebellious
Infant	Ignorant
	Confused
	Dependent
Child	Self-centered, self-absorbed
	Idealistic
	Prideful
	Low view of self
	Interdependent
Young Adult	Action/service-oriented
	Zealous
	God-centered
	Others-centered
	Mission-minded but incomplete in his or her understanding
	Independent
Parent	Intentional
	Strategic
	Reproduction-minded
	Self-feeding
	Mission-minded
	Team-minded (unity matters)
	Dependable

Typical Beliefs, Behaviors, and Attitudes of the Stage

Spiritual Stage	
Dead	Disbelief of the supernatural, or belief in many forms of the supernatural (multiple deities, interactions with the dead, superstitions, astrology, and so on)
	Disbelief in God (atheism) or belief in the possibility of God (agnosticism) or belief in a different God (member of a cult or the occult)
	Belief in one God but many ways to get to Him
	Anger toward Christians or the church or family
	Confusion about God, Jesus, and the church
	Ignorance regarding biblical truth (spiritually blind)
	Belief that the answers they are seeking lie in worldly prestige, power, fame, and so on
	Belief that they are as good as anyone else so they don't need a Savior
	Belief that they have done too much wrong so fear they can't be saved
Infant	Ignorance about what they need and what the Bible says about life and the purpose of a Christian
	Ignorance about or frustration toward Christianity and the church
	Belief that Christians make no mistakes; unrealistic expectations of themselves
	Belief that they are defined as the culture would define them
	Worldly perspective about life with some spiritual truth mixed in
Child	Excitement over having deep relationships
	Disillusionment because of their high expectations of others
	Belief that feelings are most important, which leads to spiritual highs and lows
	Lack of wisdom about how to use what they are learning — for example, too aggressive when sharing their faith, or too legalistic in their approach to dealing with their friends and family
	Belief that people are not caring for them enough
	Tendency to mimic mature Christians' behaviors in order to look good and gain praise
	Tendency to serve others in a ministry as long as the benefit outweighs the cost
	Enthusiasm about new teachings
	Confusion and unyielding nature regarding complex issues because they have an incomplete view of biblical subjects
	More knowledge about what Christians say than what the Word says

Young Adult	Desire to serve others for others' good and the glory of God
	Tendency to feel responsible for how others respond to the message; possible pride if a person accepts their message and possible discouragement if they don't
	Desire to serve but not strategic about how to train others
	Naivety about other believers — for example, they believe that others are on fire for Jesus because everyone seems to be "fine" at church
	Tendency to be black-and-white about what should happen in a church
Parent	Ability to think in terms of what a team (rather than an individual) can do
	A coaching mindset
	Desire to see the people they work with mature and become fellow workers who love them but aren't dependent on them to complete the mission

The Spiritual Needs of the Stage

Spiritual Stage	
Dead	A secure relationship with a mature believer
	A picture of the real Jesus lived out in front of them
	Answers, evidences for Christianity
	An explanation of the gospel message
	An invitation to receive Christ
Infant	Individual attention from a spiritual parent
	Protection
	An explanation of the truths (new truths) found in the Word of God
	An explanation and modeling of the habits of a growing believer
Child	A spiritual family
	Help for how to start feeding themselves
	Teaching about who they are in Christ
	Teaching about how to have a relationship with Christ
	Teaching about how to have relationships with other believers
	Teaching about appropriate expectations concerning other believers

Young Adult	A place to learn to serve
	A spiritual parent who will debrief them about ministry experiences
	Ongoing relationships that offer encouragement and accountability
	Help for establishing boundaries
	Guidance regarding appropriate expectations of people they will serve
	Help in identifying their gifts
	Skills training
Parent	An ongoing relationship with co-laborers
	A church family
	Encouragement

The Phrase from the Stage

Spiritual Stage	
Dead	"I don't believe there is a God."
	"The Bible is just a bunch of myths."
	"Evolution explains away a need for God."
	"I am not a Christian because Christians are responsible for all the wars in history."
	"There are many ways to get to God."
	"I am a Christian because I go to church and I am a good person."
	"I have been a good person, so I will be okay."
Infant	"I believe in Jesus, but my church is when I'm in the woods or on the lake."
	"I don't have to go to church to be a Christian."
	"I gave my life to Jesus and I go to church, but I don't need to be close to other people."
	"People have hurt me, so it's just me and God."
	"I don't have time to be in relationship with another Christian."
	"My spouse is my accountability partner. I don't need anyone else."
	"I pray and read my Bible. That is good enough for me."
	"My ministry is my work. I provide for my family. I don't have time for the church."
	"I didn't know the Bible said that."

Child	"I love my small group; don't add any more people to it."
	"Who are all these people coming to my church? Tell them to go somewhere else!"
	"I am not coming to church anymore. It has become too big; it has too many people."
	"My small group is not taking care of my needs."
	"I don't have anyone who is spending enough time with me; no one is discipling me."
	"I didn't like the music today. If only they did it like . . ."
	"I am not being fed in my church, so I am going to a church that meets my needs better."
Young Adult	"I love my group, but there are others who need a group like this."
	"I think I could lead a group with a little help. I have three friends I have been witnessing to, and this group would be too big for them."
	"Look how many are at church today — it's awesome! I had to walk two blocks from the closest parking spot."
	"Randy and Rachel missed group and I called to see if they are okay. Their kids have the flu, so maybe our group can make meals for them. I'll start."
	"In my devotions, I came across something I have a question about."
	"I noticed that we don't have an old folks' visitation team. Do you think I could be involved?"
Parent	People talk about what they love. When spiritual parents talk about what God is doing with them, it is not bragging or name-dropping. Humility is evident.
	"This guy at work asked me to explain the Bible to him. Pray for me."
	"We get to baptize someone from our small group tonight. When is the next 101 class? I want to get her plugged into ministry somewhere."
	"Our small group is going on a mission trip, and I have given each person a different responsibility."
	"I realize discipleship happens at home, too. Will you hold me accountable to spend time discipling my kids?"
	"I have a person in my small group who is passionate about children. Can you have the children's ministry people call me?"

leader's guide

As the small-group leader, it is your job to facilitate discussion each week. Help group members probe their beliefs and experiences using God's Word for direction. The exchange of ideas within your small group is as much a learning tool in your journey as this leader's guide is.

At the outset, it is important to get a commitment from group members to attend consistently, arrive on time, and come prepared with homework completed. The time commitment for homework each week is twenty to thirty minutes a day for five days. If this time commitment is met consistently, members will not only come prepared for your group discussions but also reinforce a daily devotional habit over the twelve weeks of the study. You should emphasize that it is important to complete each learning exercise before moving forward. Sections should not be skipped. You should also exhort members not to cram the week's lessons in just before coming to your small group for discussion.

TEAM GOALS

Each week you will be given a set of team goals that should guide the purpose and direction of your discussion for the week. You will also be given a game plan to guide your team through the material. Below is a breakdown of what a meeting will entail.

Warm-Ups: Welcome, Sharing, and Shepherding 15 minutes

It is important that you as the group leader intentionally build a relational environment within your small group and maintain it each week. This first fifteen minutes each week is dedicated to the goal of building relationships and caring for one another. This time will provide a context for members to continue sharing their stories in a safe and encouraging environment.

Build a relational environment in which each member feels safe to share. You should take some time each week to have members share parts of their personal stories. Each week you will be given questions to facilitate that discussion. Encourage members to participate in the discussion by sharing their own lives and engaging one another with follow-up questions and responses.

10 minutes

Vision Casting and Review

The context of this vision casting and review is discipleship. Keep this squarely in mind as you use this time to ask such questions as:

1. Why are we here?
2. Where are we going?
3. What have we learned so far?

45 minutes

Coaching and Practice

This is the meat of each week's discussion. During this discussion, you should be unpacking the week's lesson, including all of the activities, and evaluating how you played the game that week.

1. Where were your successes?
2. Where do you need improvement individually or as a group?
3. What are the next steps to that improvement?

The questions you should ask during this time are provided directly from the material, but each question will take your group in unique directions.

20 minutes

Game Plan and Strategy

This is your time to strategize for growth. Coach one another to grow through encouragement, constructive critique, correction, prayer, and accountability.

This may seem like a lot to cover. The guidelines are based on the assumption that you will be meeting for at least ninety minutes each week, that members will arrive on time, and that you as a leader will respect members' commitment by ending on time. If you agree to meet for a longer period of time, that's great. The material provided in this leader's guide is meant to help you cover all of the important material from the training manual. However, these questions and activities are a starting point and reinforce the main ideas of each week's study but do not prohibit you from adding your own questions or curtailing questions and activities as the Holy Spirit leads you.

It is important that you as the facilitator draw each member into the discussion to the best of your ability. The group experience will be life-changing to the degree each member participates wholeheartedly and shares openly.

Post-Practice Coach's Evaluation

This section is for you only and should help you process the group's progress. This section asks you to evaluate the players on your team in areas of progress and growth:

1. Where is each person at in the discipleship process?
2. What is each person's next step?

3. As the coach, what is your part in the process?
4. List action items or prayer points for each person.

You should provide your own notebook to make these notations in. Do not make them directly on the pages of this leader's guide for all to see. These are your private observations. Make sure you plan time for following up on this evaluation before, during, or after each week's meeting. Remember, you are discipling this team. Growth will not happen by chance. Keep your destination in mind as you grow in being an intentional leader, building a relational environment, and using the reproducible process.

Week 1:
A Heart to Make Disciples

Team goals:

1. Each member will be able to defend making disciples as a priority for both the individual Christian and the local church.
2. Each member will evaluate his or her past participation in making disciples.

Warm-Ups: Welcome, Sharing, and Shepherding   15 minutes

Have members share their stories by having them do one of the following:

- Introduce themselves and give a brief explanation of the ministry they are a part of and the role they play in that ministry
- Briefly describe their most meaningful ministry experience and why it was meaningful
- Introduce themselves and tell the group why they are participating in this study and what they hope to get out of it

Open the rest of the meeting with prayer. Pray for God to meet each member's needs for growth as both a disciple and a discipler over the next twelve weeks.

Vision Casting and Review   10 minutes

If Christianity is a team sport and the church is Christ's team, what would winning be? What is the church supposed to be and do to win?

Coaching and Practice   45 minutes

1. What part is the church commanded to play in making disciples?
2. What is your personal role, as commanded in God's Word, in helping the church make disciples?
3. Tell the group about an encounter you had sharing with someone about the church's first priority of making disciples. Were you challenged to defend this point of view?

4. How does Jesus' example and John 17 provide that defense?
5. How would you know when your work with someone you were discipling was complete?
6. How can our work of making disciples be completed and yet the process continue on until Jesus returns?
7. What three reasons did you give for why the church in America is not overcoming the Enemy?

20 minutes

Game Plan and Strategy

If Christianity is a team sport, the team cannot win unless everyone gets "in the game." Have someone read 1 Corinthians 12:14-20 aloud, and then as a group, answer the following questions:

1. Where did you place your "X" on the field diagram? Why do you think you have spent most of the last two years in that place?
2. Look again at this week's key verse, Matthew 28:18-20. How has your understanding of making disciples changed?

Close the meeting with prayer. Ask each member of the group to participate in the prayer by praying for one or more needs of another member as they were shared.

Post-Practice Coach's Evaluation

1. How did each member evaluate his or her past participation in the discipleship process?
2. What is each person's next step?
3. As their coach, what is your part in the process?
4. List action items or prayer points for each person.

Week 2:
What Is a Disciple?

Team goals:

1. Each member of the group will be able to define what a disciple is according to Matthew 4:19.
2. Based on self-assessment, each member will create an action plan to move his or her own discipleship forward in one part of the process.

15 minutes

Warm-Ups: Welcome, Sharing, and Shepherding

Open the meeting with prayer. Then open up this part of the meeting by asking the group the following questions:

1. Are you struggling to get the assignments finished?

2. Do you have a regular rhythm in your interactions with the Lord?
3. Share with the group one area of strength in your time spent with Jesus and one area of weakness.

Vision Casting and Review
10 minutes

A team cannot win unless they have the same definition of winning. Reflecting on Brandon's experience with visiting churches, what happens when church leaders don't have the same definition of discipleship?

1. How did you define disciple in this lesson?
2. When you read Luke 5:1-11, what areas did you identify that need to change to match Jesus' definition of His disciples?

Coaching and Practice
45 minutes

1. What did the story of Zacchaeus (see Luke 19:1-10; John 21:15-19; Matthew 28:19-20) say about Jesus' mission?
2. All week we have been learning that "Follow me, . . . and I will make you fishers of men" is the biblical definition of what a disciple is. Can you explain it in your own words?
3. What is the head-level change that must take place in a disciple of Jesus?
4. What is the heart-level change?
5. What is the hands-level change?

Game Plan and Strategy
20 minutes

1. As you considered your schedule, time, and money on day 5, where did you place your "X" as someone who follows Jesus, is being changed by Jesus, and is committed to the mission of Jesus?
2. Share your action plan from this week with the group.

Close the meeting with prayer. Ask each member of the group to participate in the prayer by praying for one or more needs of another member as they were shared.

Post-Practice Coach's Evaluation

1. Where did each member of the group place their "X" as someone who follows Jesus, is being changed by Jesus, and is committed to the mission of Jesus?
2. What was their action plan for growth?
3. As their coach, what is your part in the process?
4. List action items or prayer points for each person.

Week 3:
How Disciples Grow

Team goals:

1. Each member of the group will be able to name the stages of growth for a disciple.
2. Each member of the group will be able to describe the basic characteristics and needs of each growth stage of discipleship.
3. Each member of the group will be able to generally identify what growth stage their small-group members are in based on key phrases they tend to use.

15 minutes

Warm-Ups: Welcome, Sharing, and Shepherding

Open the meeting with prayer. Then ask the group the following questions:

1. What if you had never heard the gospel?
2. Where do you think you would be if you were completely ignorant of God's desire to restore a relationship with you?

10 minutes

Vision Casting and Review

One of Jesus' most profound sayings is "No one can see the kingdom of God unless he is born again" (John 3:3).

1. What were we like when we were first born to our biological mothers?
2. What similarities can you think of between our first birth and being born again?

45 minutes

Coaching and Practice

1. What are the characteristics of the spiritually dead, spiritual infant, spiritual child, spiritual young adult, and spiritual parent?
2. What are some of the typical phrases used by disciples at each of these stages?
3. What are some of the needs of a disciple at each spiritual stage?

20 minutes

Game Plan and Strategy

1. As you review the characteristics of each of these stages, which of them apply to you?
2. What are some ways you can take the next step in your own spiritual growth?
3. Lone Rangers either give up or fall into sin because they are isolated. Without the encouragement and accountability of others, our health as a disciple is at risk. Even the most mature disciple can get discouraged. Knowing this, what should a spiritually mature parent work to maintain?

In week 1, you identified the names of family, friends, and acquaintances who were spiritually dead. As a small group, support one another by closing your meeting with prayer for the needs of these individuals.

Post-Practice Coach's Evaluation

1. What stages did each member of the group identify as applying to them?
2. What next step of growth did each member of the group identify for themselves?
3. As their coach, what is your part in the process?
4. List action items or prayer points for each person.

Week 4:
Three Keys to Making Disciples

Team goals:

1. Each member of the group will be able to identify the keys for a successful discipleship journey.
2. Each member will be able to summarize the process of disciple-making.

Warm-Ups: Welcome, Sharing, and Shepherding   15 minutes

This week moves from the *why* of disciple-making to the *how*.

1. Share your observations from Acts 2:42-46 from day 1 of this week with the group.
2. Share with the group how you have experienced each part of this process (intentional leader, relational environment, and reproducible process) to date or why you believe you have not experienced them.

Vision Casting and Review   10 minutes

This is a transition week. Spend some time in a quick review before going forward. Draw a blank discipleship wheel and have the group fill it in with what you have learned so far.

Coaching and Practice   45 minutes

1. Define how the material described each of the following: an intentional leader, a relational environment, and a reproducible process.
2. What can happen if a disciple skips a stage of growth or bypasses a phase in the process?
3. According to Matthew 28:18-20, what was Jesus' attitude about His disciples' release? How had Jesus prepared them for this day? What did He say to give confidence to them?

Game Plan and Strategy   20 minutes

1. What might hinder you from being an intentional leader or creating a relational environment for those you disciple?
2. Share with the group the prayer you wrote to God on day 3 about removing those roadblocks.

3. Work on building the relationships in your current small group. Share the personal affirmations you wrote for each person in your group.
4. What holds you back from making three disciple-makers in the next five years?

Close your meeting by praying for one another according to what was shared in the responses above.

Post-Practice Coach's Evaluation

1. List the hindrances each member listed that could keep him or her from being an intentional leader or creating a relational environment.
2. What is each person's next step?
3. As their coach, what is your part in the process?
4. List action items or prayer points for each person.

Week 5:
How to Be an Intentional Leader

Team goals:

1. Each member will be challenged to grow and maintain a biblical worldview.
2. Each member will understand the three roles of an intentional leader.
3. Each member will be equipped to accurately evaluate their players.
4. Each member will be able to identify God's part, their part, and the disciple's part of the process.

15 minutes

Warm-Ups: Welcome, Sharing, and Shepherding

In week 5, an analogy is made between Little League sports and discipleship. Did you play sports as a child? Who taught you your favorite sport or hobby (such as playing an instrument)? How well did your instructor know the game? As a Christian, have you benefited from an intentional leader?

10 minutes

Vision Casting and Review

Open the rest of the meeting with prayer.

Understanding the mind of God and mastering His Word are lifelong endeavors. Nevertheless, intentional leaders work continually to build a biblical worldview in order to better understand the game.

1. Where do you need to strengthen your biblical worldview?
2. Which of the statements from this week would you struggle to explain to a new believer?

Coaching and Practice   45 minutes

1. Summarize in one sentence what intentional leadership is.
2. What is the difference in *program* thinking and *person* thinking in making disciples?
3. What does Ephesians 4:12 show us about the leader's role?
4. List three things a coach should look for when evaluating a team.
5. What are the two keys to knowing your players/disciples?
6. Why is it important to distinguish between God's part, our part, and the disciple's part?

Game Plan and Strategy   20 minutes

1. Share with the group the rankings you gave yourself for the three roles Jesus used with His disciples: teaching, modeling, and challenging.
2. What changes do you need to make to spend more time with those God has placed in your life who need to be discipled?
3. What can you do to create more relationship with those you are discipling?
4. Share how you evaluated yourself and how your friend evaluated you in the areas of awareness, responsiveness, and empathy.
5. Which of the three do you need to work on?

Close your meeting by praying for one another according to what was shared in the responses above.

Post-Practice Coach's Evaluation

1. Take note of how each member ranked and evaluated themselves in answer to the "game plan" questions.
2. What is each person's next step?
3. As their coach, what is your part in the process?
4. List action items or prayer points for each person.

Week 6:
A Closer Look at a Relational Environment

Team goals:

1. Each member of the group will be able to identify the key components of a relational environment.
2. Each member will be equipped to create a relational environment.
3. Each member will be challenged to overcome his or her own personal obstacles to creating a relational environment.

15 minutes

Warm-Ups: Welcome, Sharing, and Shepherding

On day 1 of this week, you were asked to identify general but relational information about each of your fellow members. If you completed the list well, you already know the value of being relational. If you couldn't complete the list, take some time this week to hear a little of each other's stories.

10 minutes

Vision Casting and Review

Open the rest of the meeting with prayer.

1. What are two benefits of growing as a group instead of in isolation?
2. Look back at 1 John 1:7. What do you think "walk in the Light" means?
3. What do you think might hinder you from being transparent in a disciple-making group, and what can you do to overcome those fears and obstacles?

45 minutes

Coaching and Practice

1. According to the Scripture references given on day 2 of this week, what can you do to create a safe environment?
2. Which of these acts of shepherding have you experienced in a small group?
3. Which have you wanted to experience but did not?
4. What could you do to help you keep your heart right about shepherding the people in your group?
5. How did you rank your efforts in bringing back the strays?
6. Consider Jim's experience at the hospital from day 5. How would you feel if you were the person lying in the hospital bed?
7. What would you think if you were the nurse in charge?

20 minutes

Game Plan and Strategy

A relational environment meets spiritual needs, but it meets physical needs as well. That was part of what attracted others to the disciples in the book of Acts. People outside the church witnessed a caring community that did more than talk; they shared their possessions, their time, and their energy meeting needs. A disciple-maker does this as well, leading growing disciples to serve each other in tangible ways. The result is often other people who become interested in following Jesus. How can you improve in this area?

Close your meeting by praying for one another according to what was shared in the responses above.

Post-Practice Coach's Evaluation

1. As you discuss improving your relational environment, take note of each member's ideas.
2. As you have observed each member of your group, what do you believe is each person's next step?

3. As their coach, what is your part in the process?
4. List action items or prayer points for each person.

Week 7:
A Closer Look at the Reproducible Process

Team goals:

1. Each member of the group will be equipped with a reproducible process of spiritual growth.
2. Each member will understand how to minister to small-group members who are at each of the different places in the discipleship process of Share, Connect, Minister, or Disciple.

Warm-Ups: Welcome, Sharing, and Shepherding   15 minutes

Open the rest of the meeting with prayer.

1. As you look at the overview of the reproducible process, how intentional have you been as a disciple-maker?
2. Share your experience at explaining the SCMD process to someone.

Vision Casting and Review   10 minutes

1. What are the four parts of the reproducible discipleship process?
2. How would Christianity have been affected if Philip had not been discipled and released to go and make disciples himself?

Coaching and Practice   45 minutes

1. Read John 4:4-30 aloud. What are the four things Jesus shares with the woman at the well?
2. Do you believe that God made you for relationships? How does the belief that being a disciple is just about us and Jesus directly contradict Jesus' command in Mark 12:29-30?
3. Using 1 John 4:19-21 as your foundation, what would you say to a believer who said that he or she did not need other people to be rightly related to God?
4. What is the third connection disciples need to make after connecting to God and other believers?
5. Review the story of the feeding of the five thousand and discuss what jobs Jesus gave the disciples.
6. What do you think is "the work" Jesus was finishing?
7. Take a moment and read Acts 1:1-11 aloud. What did it look like for Peter, Philip, and Timothy to "go and make disciples"?

20 minutes

Game Plan and Strategy

1. Share with the group your self-evaluation of the frequency and depth of your relationship with God.
2. What fears, insecurities, struggles, and doubts do you need to give over to the Lord so you can be a more effective disciple-maker?
3. Share your list of names you believe God has empowered you to disciple.
4. Pray with one another, asking God to lead each of you in discipling those on your lists.

Close your meeting by praying for one another according to what was shared in the responses above.

Post-Practice Coach's Evaluation

1. What specifics did group members share from their self-evaluations of their relationships with God? Make special note of their fears, insecurities, struggles, and doubts.
2. Using God's Word as a guide, what do you believe is each person's next step?
3. How can you encourage, exhort, or even admonish each member in love to help him or her grow?
4. List action items or prayer points for each person.

Week 8:
Share: Being Intentional with the Spiritually Dead and Spiritual Infants

Team goals:

1. Each group member will know how to share with the spiritually dead.
2. Members will be challenged to practice sharing their own lives with others.
3. Members will practice sharing the gospel and biblical truth with others.
4. Members will be equipped to share new spiritual habits with others.

15 minutes

Warm-Ups: Welcome, Sharing, and Shepherding

Open the rest of the meeting with prayer.

When you share with spiritually dead people, they might disagree with your answers to their questions, but they cannot disagree with what God has done in your life. Share your testimony with the group.

10 minutes

Vision Casting and Review

The focus of this week was on what the disciple-maker does at each stage of growth — the reproducible process. Read 1 Peter 3:15 aloud and summarize the three directions Peter gives us.

Coaching and Practice   45 minutes

1. What do the spiritually dead need?
2. What do you think are the top three questions unbelievers struggle to understand?
3. What are the biblical answers to those questions?
4. Pair members of your small group and role-play sharing the gospel with one another.
5. Sharing the gospel is only the beginning. We share with spiritual infants by opening our lives to them. Review Jesus' example of sharing His life (see Luke 5:27-32; 7:36-50; 11:38-42) from day 3. Share your observations of what Jesus did as an intentional leader that could be considered sharing His life with His disciples.
6. Explain how you can assess a spiritual infant's needs in the areas of the Bible, prayer, and fellowship.
7. Share the Bible-reading plan you developed on day 5 and discuss whether or not it would be a successful plan for a spiritual infant.
8. What reasons does the writer of Hebrews give for regular church attendance?

Game Plan and Strategy   20 minutes

1. Share the three things you want to improve in order to better disciple a spiritual infant.
2. Throughout this training manual, we have given you tools and challenges to not only make disciples but be a disciple. Where do you want to improve in your walk with Christ?

Close your meeting by praying for one another according to what was shared in the responses above.

Post-Practice Coach's Evaluation

1. Take note of each member's response to the question "Where do you want to improve in your walk with Christ?"
2. What is each person's next step?
3. As their coach, what is your part in the process?
4. List action items or prayer points for each person.

Week 9:
Connect: Helping Spiritual Children Grow

Team goals:

1. Each group member will know how to help the spiritual infant connect.
2. Members will be challenged to connect with their disciples relationally.
3. Members will understand how to connect spiritual infants with God the Father, their family the church, and God's purpose.

4. Members will be challenged to evaluate their own connections to God, the church, and God's purpose.

15 minutes   Warm-Ups: Welcome, Sharing, and Shepherding

Open the rest of the meeting with prayer.

1. Recall Doug's story from day 1. Do you relate more easily to the experience of Brandon and Jim or to Doug?
2. Which of the descriptions from day 1 accurately reflects your walk with Christ?

10 minutes   Vision Casting and Review

1. List from memory the three connections an intentional leader helps a spiritual infant or child make.
2. Share your list of ways you can be more intentional with the spiritual children God has placed in your life in order to help them mature.

45 minutes   Coaching and Practice

1. What kinds of things should we model for those we disciple?
2. What do you think it looks like for Christians to feed themselves spiritually?
3. What spiritual disciplines do you consider foundational for a spiritual child to learn?
4. What potential roadblocks do you think could hinder a spiritual child's connection to God?
5. Read Hebrews 3:12-13 and 10:24-25 aloud and discuss three specific roles a small group fulfills for its members.
6. Share with the group a bit about the people you are discipling and identify ways you can help connect them more deeply with the family of the church.
7. How did you paraphrase Ephesians 4:12 on day 4?
8. What are some reasons a person may struggle connecting those they disciple to their purposes?
9. Share the name of someone you are discipling and the specific steps you can take to connect that person to his or her purpose.
10. According to the Scriptures shared in this week's lesson, what are the six steps to working through conflict?

20 minutes   Game Plan and Strategy

1. Which one of the three connections we have studied today is the most difficult for you? What can you do to improve in that area?
2. Identify a place God personally impacted you in this week's lesson. Share with the group why you think this point had such an impact. What will you do about it?
3. Consider any unresolved conflicts with those you are discipling and ask the group to hold you accountable to do your part to reconcile the situation.

4. Be specific about what God is calling you to do to resolve the conflicts.

Close your meeting by praying for one another according to what was shared in the responses above.

Post-Practice Coach's Evaluation

1. Take note of each member's responses to the "game plan" questions.
2. What is each person's next step?
3. If you become aware during this week's discussion of unresolved conflicts in the lives of your group members, specifically plan how you will hold them accountable to do their part in reconciling the situation.
4. As their coach, what is your part in the process?
5. List action items or prayer points for each person.

Week 10:
Minister: Helping Young Adults Help Others

Team goals:

1. Each member will be equipped to challenge spiritual young adults to be others-centered through ministry rather than being self-centered.
2. Each member will be prepared to identify ministry opportunities to involve young adults in.
3. Each member will understand how to come alongside a spiritual young adult as he or she transitions to ministering to others.
4. Each member will be equipped and challenged to release the spiritual adult (parent) at the appropriate time.

Warm-Ups: Welcome, Sharing, and Shepherding   15 minutes

Open the rest of the meeting with prayer.

Share your responses from "the phrase from the stage" activity. How did you identify the stages of the spiritual child versus the spiritual young adult?

Vision Casting and Review   10 minutes

1. Read Matthew 20:25-28 aloud. What did Jesus mean when He said, "Not so with you"?
2. What was God's Plan A?
3. Why do you think there was no Plan B?
4. Consider those you are discipling and share what ministry or service opportunities you could involve them in.

45 minutes

Coaching and Practice

1. Identify three things an intentional disciple-maker does to train a spiritual young adult.
2. The following are potential pitfalls for a disciple preparing to serve in ministry. Check the ones you have experienced.
   ☐ Feeling failure because nobody noticed them
   ☐ Losing motivation because no one said thank you
   ☐ Being hurt because someone criticized their efforts
   ☐ Wanting to quit because their efforts didn't measure up
   ☐ Being surprised when people had different expectations
3. Jesus prepared His disciples for extreme rejection. Reflect on Matthew 5:11-12. What motivation does Jesus tell His disciples to have so they won't give up?
4. Discuss the Scripture references used to illustrate how Jesus got His disciples "in the game." What was the ministry in each situation, and what did the disciple do?
5. What opportunities could you provide for people you disciple to involve them in ministry with you?
6. How have opportunities to "get in the game" of ministry impacted your growth?
7. Read John 15:15 aloud. How did Jesus' relationship with His disciples change?
8. Read John 20:17 aloud. How did the disicples' relationships change after Jesus' resurrection?

20 minutes

Game Plan and Strategy

Ask one another the accountability questions from day 5.

Close your meeting by praying for one another according to what was shared in the responses above.

Post-Practice Coach's Evaluation

1. List areas of accountability for each member.
2. What is each person's next step?
3. As their coach, what is your part in the process?
4. List action items or prayer points for each person.

Week 11:
Disciple: Being Intentional
with Spiritual Parents

Team goals:

1. Each member will reflect on the past twelve weeks and clearly evaluate his or her own growth and spiritual maturity.
2. Each member will be clear on what it means to bring our work "to completion" (Philippians 1:6) as the goal of his or her ministry.
3. Each member will understand how to transfer authority.

4. Each member will be confident in how to maintain relationships with spiritual parents he or she has released.

Warm-Ups: Welcome, Sharing, and Shepherding · 15 minutes

Open the rest of the meeting with prayer.

Share with the group how you would respond if someone challenged where you think you are in the discipleship process. What evidence would you give to show why you think you are at the stage you selected?

Vision Casting and Review · 10 minutes

1. How did Brandon know that the men in his small group were ready to move into their own ministries?
2. Why do you think it is hard to release a spiritual parent you have discipled?
3. Write three phrases a person in the spiritual parent stage might communicate that would help you know he or she is ready to be released. (If you need help, refer to day 5 of week 3.)

Coaching and Practice · 45 minutes

1. Discuss with your group why the disciples would have continued to be followers rather than co-leaders if Jesus had stayed with them.
2. Take a moment and review the discipleship wheel. How do the three sections in the "disciple" quadrant demonstrate the process of transferring responsibility?
3. What are the characteristics of a spiritually F.A.T. person?
4. The first step in releasing disciples is to acknowledge and recognize them as being ready to take on the discipleship role for themselves. What two things does this recognition accomplish?
5. What damage might be done if we recognize someone too soon?
6. What would you do to prepare a spiritual parent to be released to make disciples?
7. What would you intentionally do to release the spiritual parent?
8. How will you continue to relate to a spiritual parent after he or she has been released?
9. As a group, create and fill in as much of the discipleship wheel as you can from memory, looking back through the training manual only when really needed.

Game Plan and Strategy · 20 minutes

1. What will change when you release your disciple to be a spiritual parent?
2. How will you respond when your disciple makes mistakes? How about if he or she does a better job than you?
3. How can you keep your relationships fresh with the spiritual parents you have released to make disciples?
4. What fears or doubts hinder you from transferring responsibility to those you disciple? Be ready to share them with your group.

Close your meeting by praying for one another according to what was shared in the responses above.

Post-Practice Coach's Evaluation

1. Take note of each member's responses to the "game plan" questions.
2. What is each person's next step?
3. As their coach, what is your part in the process?
4. List action items or prayer points for each person.

Week 12:
One Necessary Tool:
A Small-Group Curriculum

Team goals:

1. Each member will be reminded of the biblical value of storying as a curriculum.
2. Each member will be equipped to use storying as a small-group discipleship tool.

15 minutes

Warm-Ups: Welcome, Sharing, and Shepherding

Open the rest of the meeting with prayer.

1. What is storying?
2. Why did Jesus use storying?
3. Read 1 Corinthians 10:11-12 aloud. Why did Paul use these stories?
4. What does the text say was God's reason for having these stories written down for us?

10 minutes

Vision Casting and Review

1. Recall as a group what things Rob and Jill did or did not do to create a relational environment for their small group.
2. Why do you think that leaders feel that, when leading a small-group discussion, they have to give the answers to questions asked?
3. Read James 2:22-25 aloud and discuss the difference in listening to the Word and doing it.

45 minutes

Coaching and Practice

1. Review as a group the steps outlined in this training manual for biblical storying.
2. Practice role-playing with one another by choosing a familiar Bible story and storying it for one another. (You could use Luke 5:1-11 from the week's lesson.)
3. Guiding the story into the heads, hearts, and hands of your small group requires their participation in the experience. How can you help your small group experience the story?

4. What is the difference between "head," "heart," and "hands" questions?

Game Plan and Strategy   20 minutes

1. Share with the group your experience of learning Luke 5:1-11 and storying it for someone.
2. What was most surprising to you about the process? What was most difficult?
3. What tips would you have for others who are new to storying?

Close your meeting by praying for one another according to what was shared in the responses above.

Post-Practice Coach's Evaluation

1. Where would you now place each member in the discipleship process? Use evidence you have learned to support this evaluation.
2. What is each person's next step?
3. As their coach, what is your part in the process?
4. Schedule a time for you to discuss these observations privately with each member of your group before the group officially ends.

notes

1. George Barna, *Revolution* (Carol Stream, IL: Tyndale, 2006), 32.
2. Thom S. Rainer, *The Unchurched Next Door: Understanding Faith Stages as Keys to Sharing Your Faith* (Grand Rapids, MI: Zondervan, 2003), 3.
3. Rodney Stark, *The Rise of Christianity: How the Obscure, Marginal Jesus Movement Became the Dominant Religious Force in the Western World in a Few Centuries* (New York: Harper Collins, 1996), 6.
4. If you are new to Bible reading, here are some great resources to get you started: http://www.bibleplan.org; William D. Hendricks and Howard G. Hendricks, *Living by the Book* (Chicago: Moody, 2007).
5. Statistics from the Global Research Department, International Mission Board, SBC.

authors

JIM PUTMAN is a seventeen-year ministry veteran, author, and national speaker. He is also the senior pastor of Real Life Ministries in Post Falls, Idaho. He holds degrees from Boise State University and Boise Bible College. With his background in sports, he believes in the value of strong coaching as a means to discipling. Jim lives with his wife and three sons in Post Falls.

AVERY T. WILLIS JR. is an international author, leader, speaker, and conference leader. Among other things, he serves as executive director of the International Orality Network and ambassador-at-large for the Avery T. Willis Center for Global Outreach at Oklahoma Baptist University. He received his BA from Oklahoma Baptist University and his M. Div. and Th.D. from Southwestern Baptist Theological Seminary. He currently lives in Arkansas with his wife, Shirley. The loves of their lives are their five children and sixteen grandchildren, who are dynamic Christians, plus two young great-grandchildren.

BRANDON GUINDON is the executive pastor at Real Life Ministries in Post Falls, Idaho. He, along with his team, pioneered the small-groups ministry at Real Life. His passion and privilege for the past eleven years has been to teach and train leaders from both the local and global church in how to make disciples through small groups. Brandon holds an MA in church leadership from Hope International University. He and his wife, Amber, have four children.

BILL KRAUSE is currently serving in family ministries at Real Life Ministries in Post Falls, Idaho. Previous to this post he was the professor of Christian education at Boise Bible College. He and his wife, Jill, have four children. Bill has been involved in youth, children's, and family ministry for more than twenty-seven years. He is a graduate of Puget Sound Christian College and earned his master's in education from Eastern Washington University.

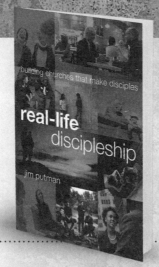
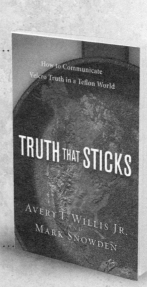
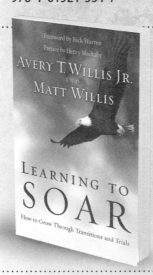